ABANDONED NORTH ALABAMA

WHERE THE STORIES ENDED

ROBERT POSEY

AMERICA
THROUGH TIME®
ADDING COLOR TO AMERICAN HISTORY

America Through Time is an imprint of Fonthill Media LLC
www.through-time.com
office@through-time.com

Published by Arcadia Publishing by arrangement with Fonthill Media LLC
For all general information, please contact Arcadia Publishing:
Telephone: 843-853-2070
Fax: 843-853-0044
E-mail: sales@arcadiapublishing.com
For customer service and orders:
Toll-Free 1-888-313-2665

www.arcadiapublishing.com

First published 2023

ISBN 978-1-63499-485-9

Typeset in Trade Gothic 10pt on 15pt
Printed and bound in England

CONTENTS

ACKNOWLEDGMENTS

Most importantly, I would like to thank my daughter, Lacey Posey, for being my sidekick through this adventure. I have never met in all my years someone as brave as you. When I was afraid to get out of the car, you pushed me. When I was too lazy to get out of bed, you motivated me. When I was ready to settle for mediocrity, you reminded me how to be a main character. I hope you never give up exploring. Just maybe start making sure you wear your respirator more often!

There would be no "Bandofam" without Carter Banks, Eric Hammon, Steve Ronin, Justin Collins, and Morgan Bryce. I can thank tons more explorers who checked out these locations with me or even just offered me motivation, but it would take up about half my word count. Exploring alone is terrifying and you turned the "I" in this book to "we."

I would like to thank the three people who never give up on me despite me giving them so many reasons to: G-diddy, Nonna, and Goosey. I know my dad is obligated to support my strange endeavors but Nonna and Goosey, do not think I have not noticed that you choose to. The minute Lacey was born the two of you became my two biggest supporters and I would be a wreck right now without your support. Thank you to the Hulsey family for feeding me.

Last but not least, thank you to my best friend, Erin. You, Maddie, and Tuck have helped me through so much since I first discovered you weren't so basic after all. I would not have finished this had it not been for you.

INTRODUCTION

Most would never stop to investigate a slight glimpse of cinder blocks covered in vines and weeds, but there is something about it that I never can ignore. I must know what was deemed something we could neglect. What is nature trying so vehemently to hide from us? The truth is, everything. We fight it for so many places, but for some reason, the protectors of some places have given up their posts. These are the things that drive my yearning to explore them. Was it a descent to hard times? Was it a death? Was it something about the place such as an obstacle too hard to overcome? A hospital I explored once was full of asbestos and the price to even demolish it was too costly for the city so it sat there with police tape waiting on its last days, which are still yet to come in this particular case.

I remember the time my ex-wife and I purchased our first house and posted it proudly on social media. I wanted to invite all my friends over and show off this place that belonged to us. Fast forward to our divorce when simply walking through the door became a constant reminder of the things that, at the time, I felt like I had lost, or possibly even taken for granted and squandered. That house made me understand a lot about my explorations. If just a divorce were to cause me such loathing over a place that I was once proud of, what could a death cause? The halls to these buildings hold memories. Hidden throughout them are stories, questions and sometimes answers tucked away neatly in places people have not looked in many years.

Avert your eyes if you are squeamish. Prepare your soul if you are prone to heartache. The answers I have found usually do not have happy endings. Should you choose to continue this journey with me, I will show you the deaths, the divorces, the failures, and the burdens that led to the resentment and neglect of places where people once found solace.

1

THE SMELL OF DEATH

We're not gonna find a dead body!" I tell my friend as we slip through the door into an office area with pamphlets about how to pick a casket, care for a loved one who just lost a spouse, and how to plan a funeral. This room is in complete disarray. The room itself is a mess but it feels as if nothing is missing and, if cleaned, could be re-opened in a week or two. A foul smell immediately hits us, making me question the certainty I had about not finding a body.

Anything death related comes with an unsettling feeling. Funeral homes, crematories, and morgues make the hair on your neck stand up whether you believe in ghosts or not. You hear noises, you feel eyes on you, and you heighten your senses to absorb everything. The noises you hear in a funeral home are no different than any other place but logic like that only comes later when you are safely driving away in your car.

We walk past the office and turn right into a hallway that has restrooms on the left and a room on the right with several seemingly brand-new caskets displayed to sell with price tags still hanging off the handles. I have been to many funeral homes but few with a collection of caskets still in pristine condition. One thing a lot of people don't realize is that when someone is cremated some funeral homes will rent a special casket for the family to hold a traditional ceremony. These rental caskets are used repeatedly and are often stained by body leakage. I have found several of these caskets in my explorations.

At the end of the hallway, we find a door leading to a paltry chapel with enough seating for thirty to fifty guests. The podium in the front is still covered with fake flowers and a microphone still sits in its stand. An out-of-tune piano just to the left of the dais can still be played but many of the keys now stick. We walked to the front of the chapel and through a set of double doors on the left to find what I came to see: a fully stocked embalming room.

The room is filled with tools, drains, tubes, pumps, and an assortment of cosmetics used to prepare the bodies for viewing and preservation. A jar of flesh-like putty used to disguise wounds and an assortment of wigs. Tools are laid out perfectly on a counter next to the embalming table that still has the positioning block laid on top of it. The garbage can at the end of the table contains blood-covered gloves, leading me to believe that when the doors to this place were closed, they were expecting them to re-open.

The stench we noticed at first disappeared by the time we got to the chapel, so we knew it came from somewhere other than the likely spots to find a body. The fear was justified as many corpses and cremains have been found in abandoned funeral homes and mortuaries, even a few cases in Alabama. As we make our way out, we noticed it was coming from the restroom.

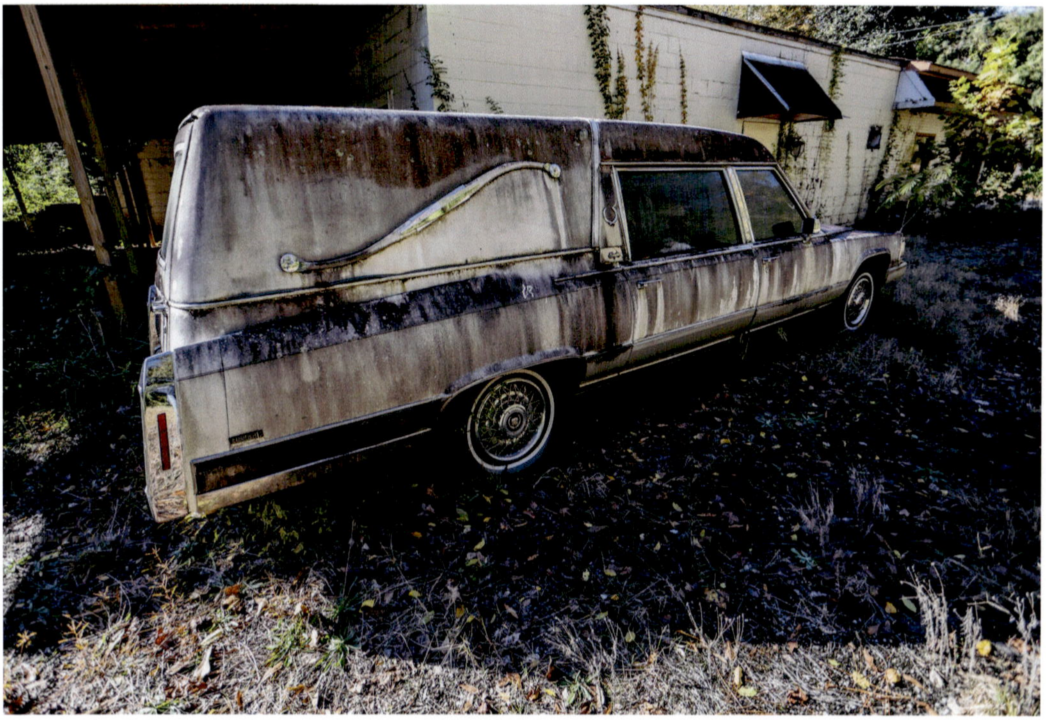

A hearse exposed to the elements sits outside the funeral home.

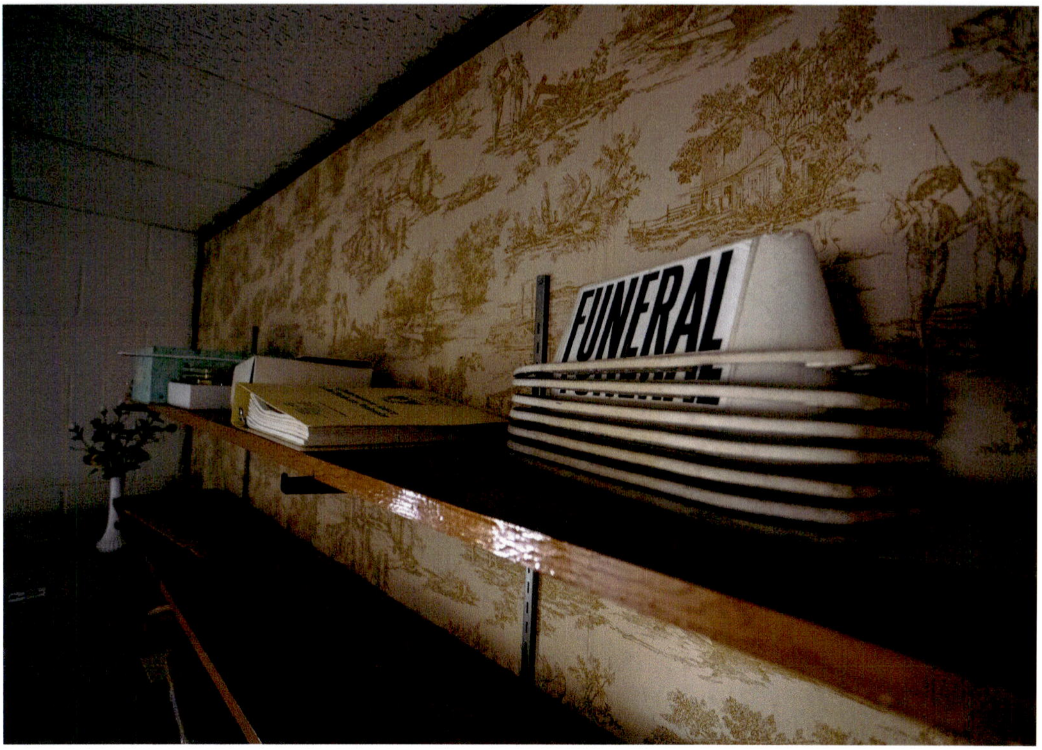

Inside the still relatively organized office.

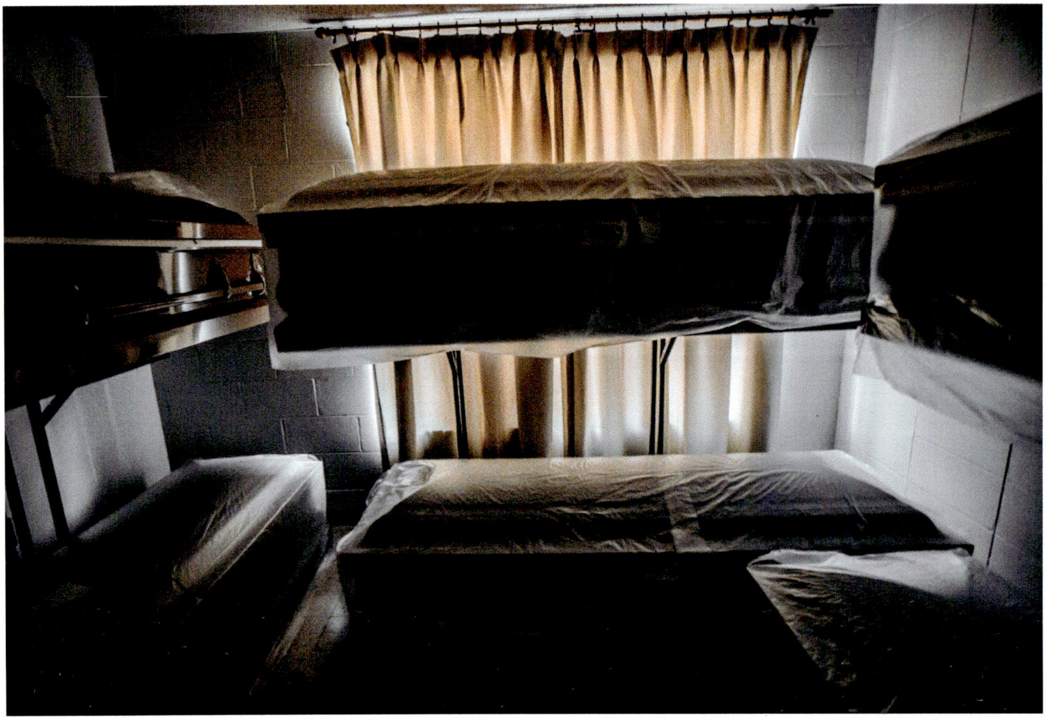

Caskets still displayed with price tags.

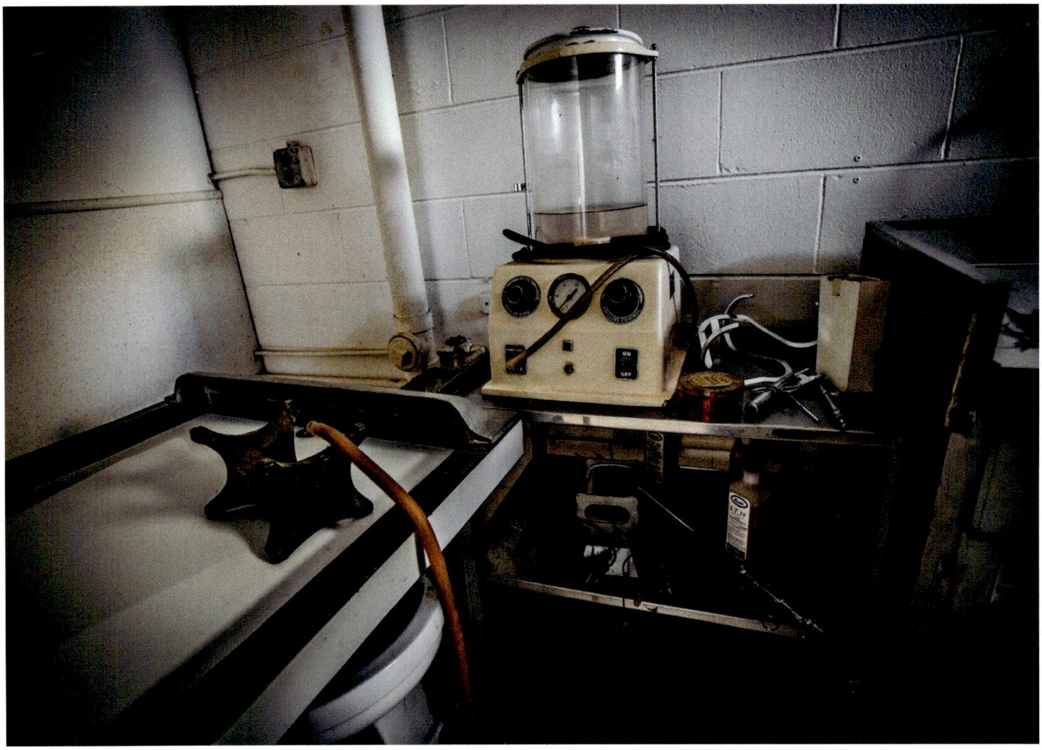

A positioning block sits on the embalming table.

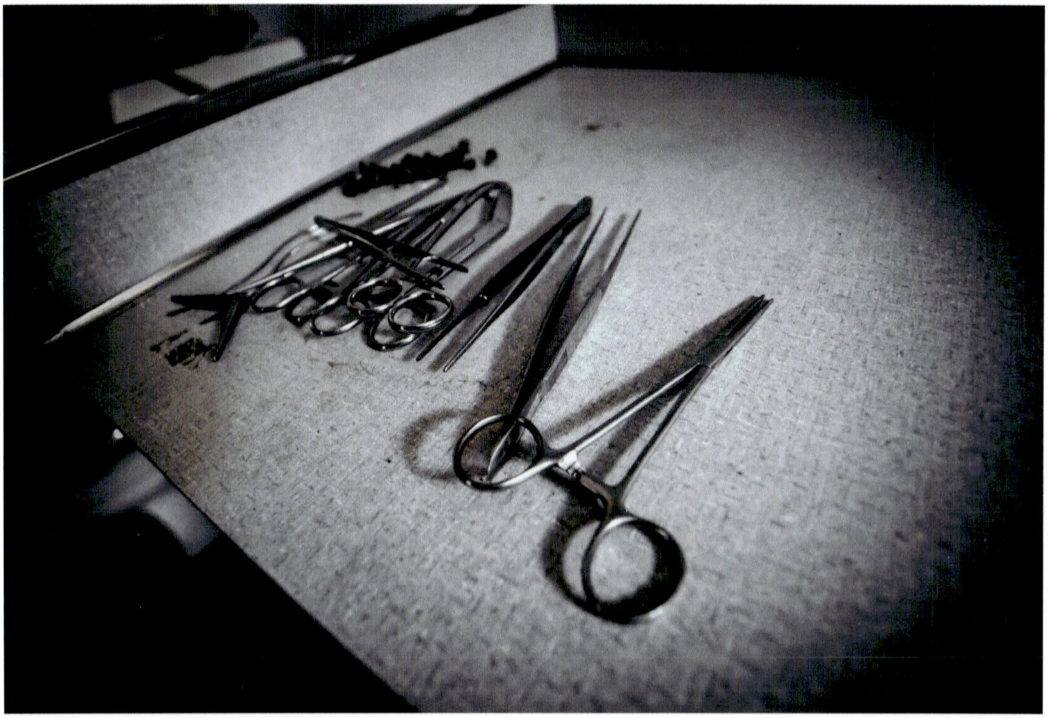

Tools are still laid out on the counter.

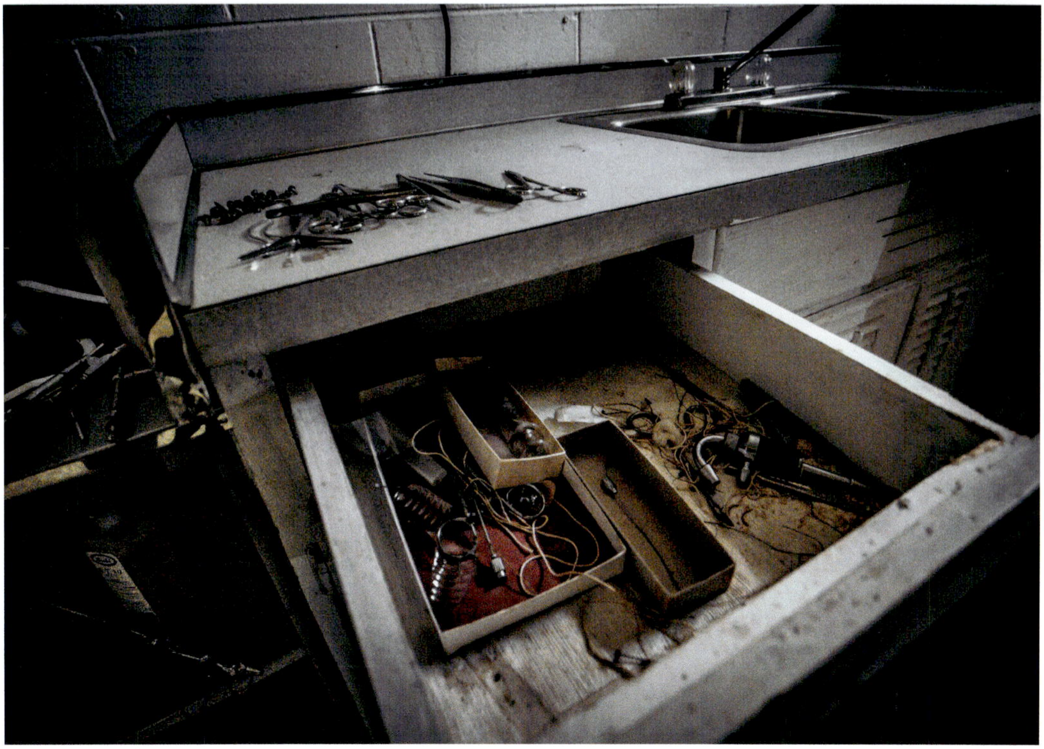

More of the mortician's tools inside a drawer.

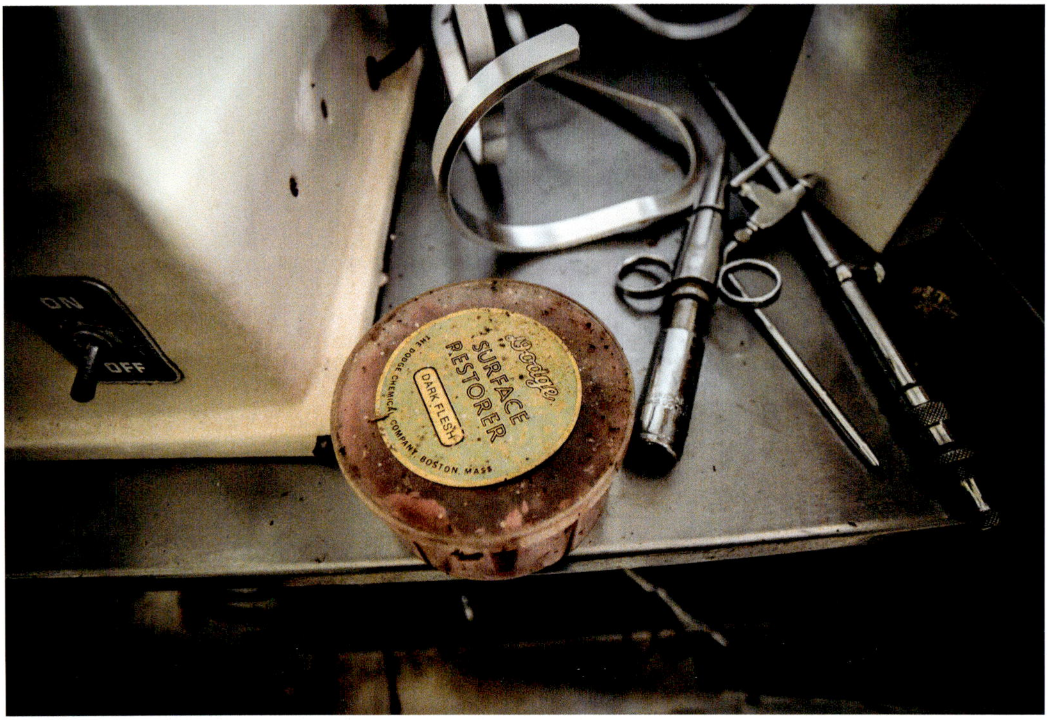

Surface restorer used to cover up blemishes before the mortician applies makeup.

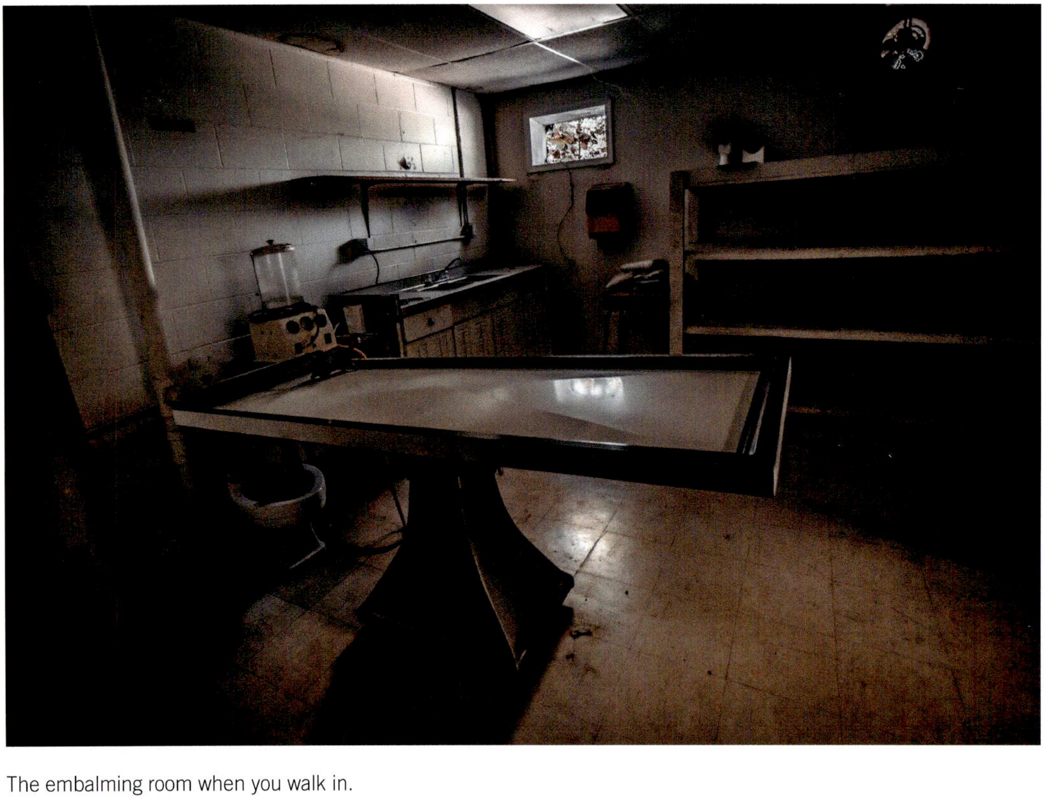

The embalming room when you walk in.

2

THE THEATER ON A HILL

People will give me locations and tell me stories about houses quite frequently but rarely does what actually happened line up with the tales they have been sharing for years. I will go to these places and find nothing. Sometimes there is not even a sign there was ever something there. When someone tells me one of these stories, I almost always follow up and hunt it down.

This story came as a surprise. There is a popular abandoned house with a beautiful aesthetic that even people who do not consider themselves urban or rural explorers photograph frequently. Having never seen it in person, it was a must-stop while in the area. I asked a local gas station attendant if he knew anything about the old home. The story he told me fascinated me so much that we decided to plan a whole day on this property. He told me of the man who lived there and the huge reputation he had in the town.

The owner of the house for many years was a preacher. He was also a sheep farmer but spent much of his time organizing and putting on a live nativity scene with local actors and live animals for his community. This was a massive production, especially for just one man to accomplish. The shows, according to locals, began in the early 1970s and continued into the 1990s when the man's health deteriorated, and he was unable to continue. The popularity of the shows led to esteemed local guests including Alabama's first elected republican governor whose role ended up causing a scene of its own. An angry audience member reportedly ran into the scene and grabbed a doll representing baby Jesus. He then threw the doll at the governor and yelled, "Here governor! Hold baby Jesus for a photo!"

The impressive amphitheater rests near the old home at the very top of a hill now covered in brush and tall trees. There is a small driveway, but it is so overgrown that taking a vehicle to the top would damage the paint on it. When you get to the top of the hill, you still have to walk about 50 yards through thick brush to arrive at the incredible amphitheater.

There are not many signs indicating the spectacle this place once was. Immediately when you walk up, you see on the ground a sign for the nativity and the first building you come to houses a giant throne now starting to fall apart. A hole in the ceiling lets water and brush in and you can see on the ground where the water has been collecting for a long time. I walked past the first building and found a truly amazing site. Nestled deep in the woods hidden completely was a huge, tiered amphitheater with concrete step seating.

This incredible feat, accomplished by a single incredibly determined man, would likely never be seen again if not for locals telling the story to anyone who would listen. I was not a family member and I had never met the men in that gas station but the legacy this preacher left was enough to share with a complete stranger. Our stories will die soon after us unless you make an impact on people in the way this man did. His life may have ended but his story was one of the astonishing ones that carries on well after his death.

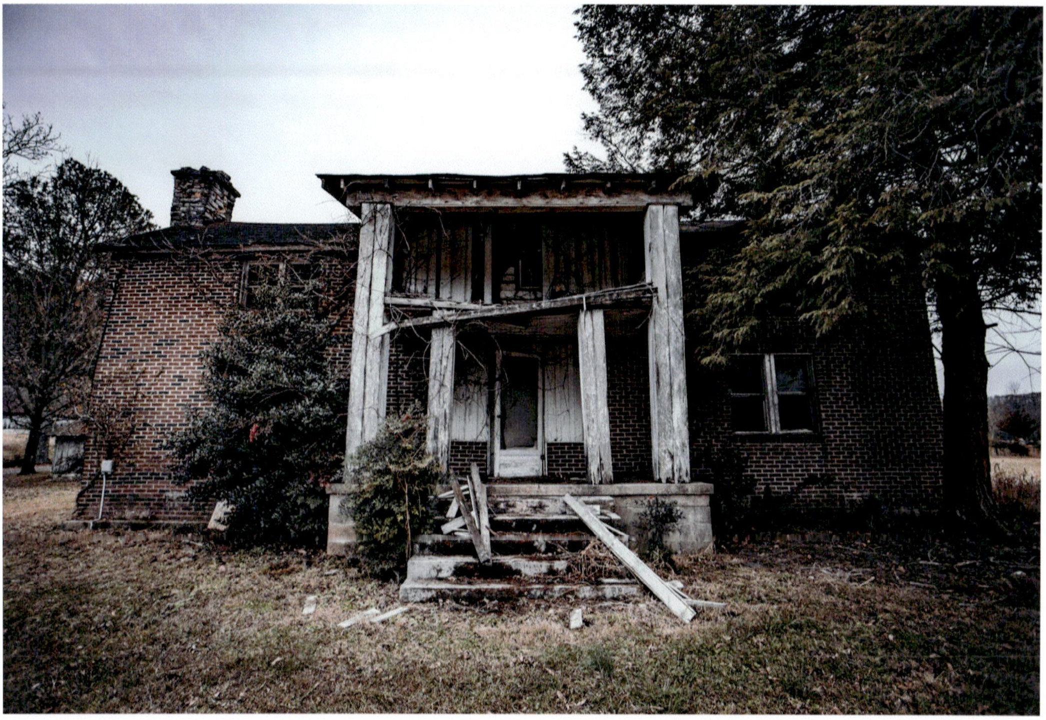

The preacher's old house is a popular spot for photographers in North Alabama.

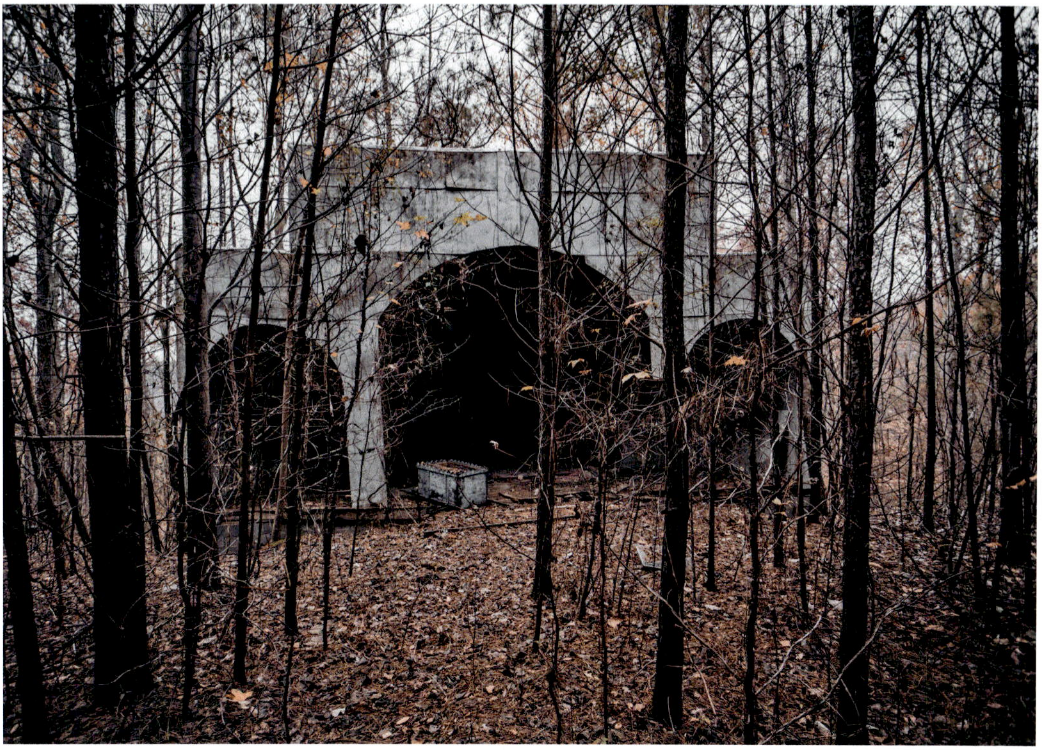

The first thing you see when walking to the amphitheater is this building where the throne sits.

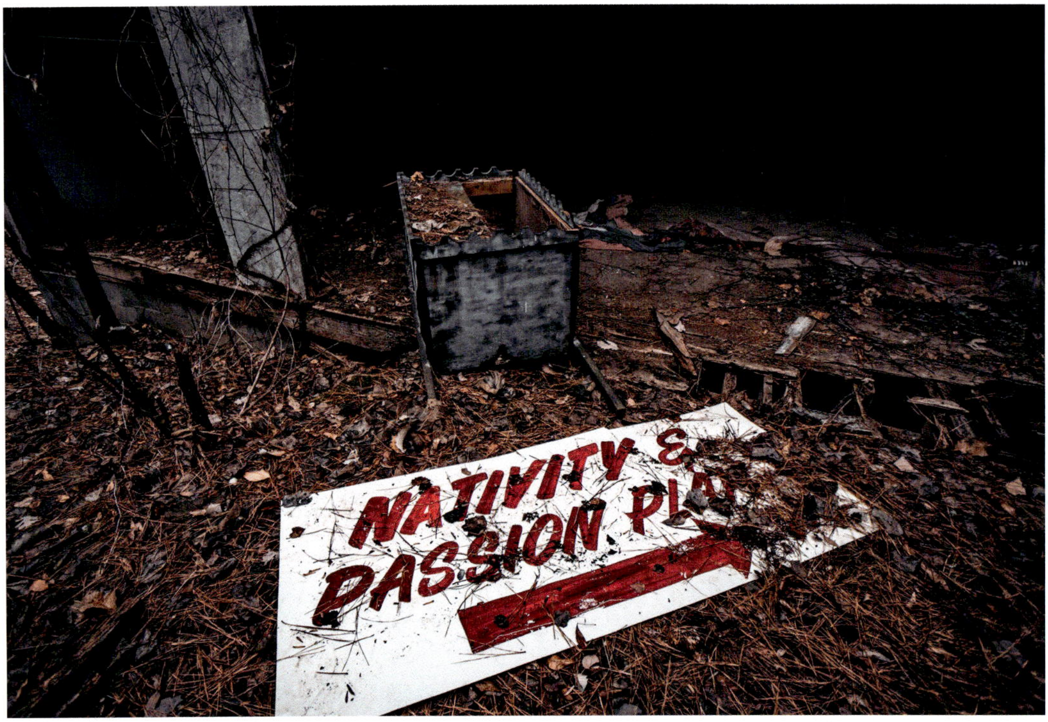

A sign leading to the nativity scene still sits on the ground as soon as you walk up.

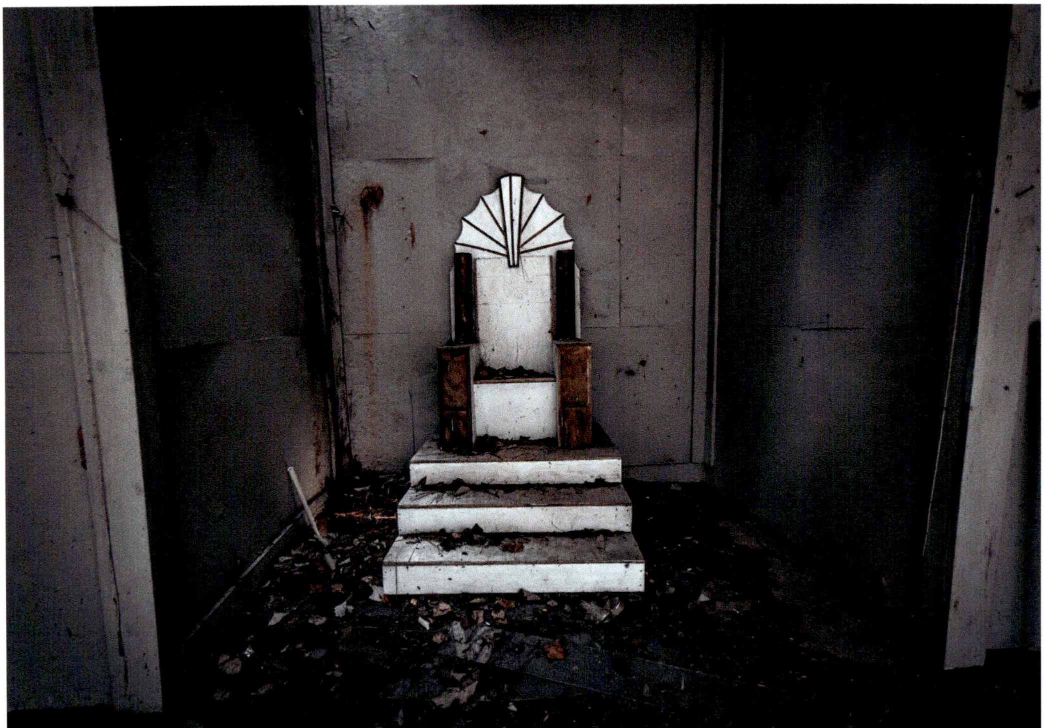

The throne now sits surrounded by debris from the roof.

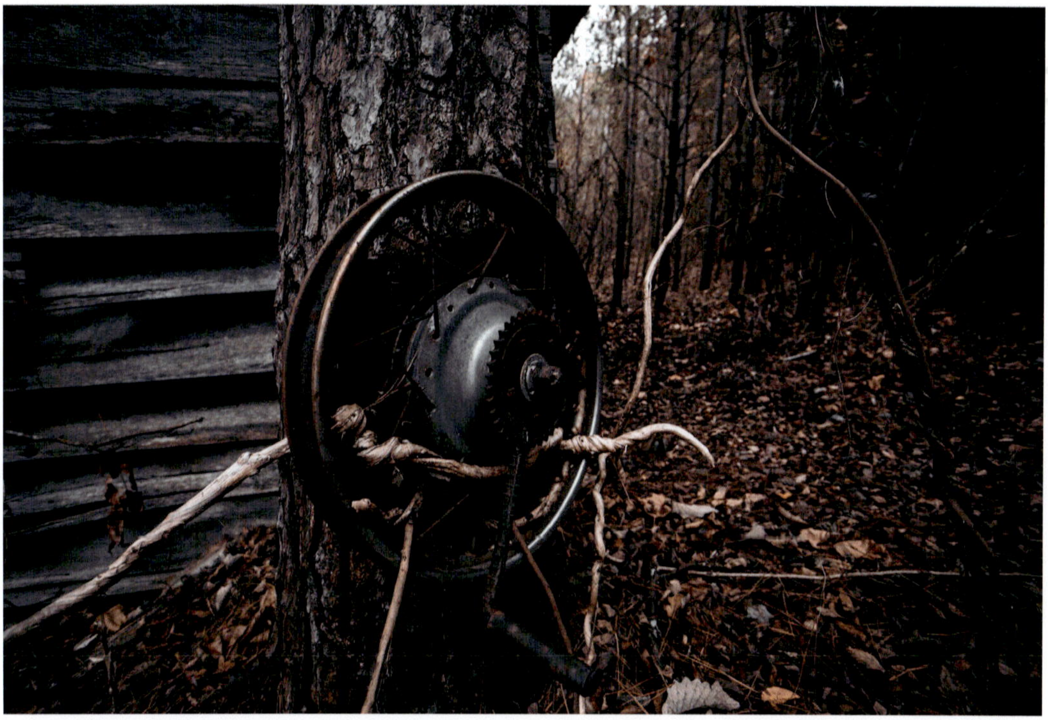

A homemade gear attached to a tree; I could not figure out what the preacher used this for.

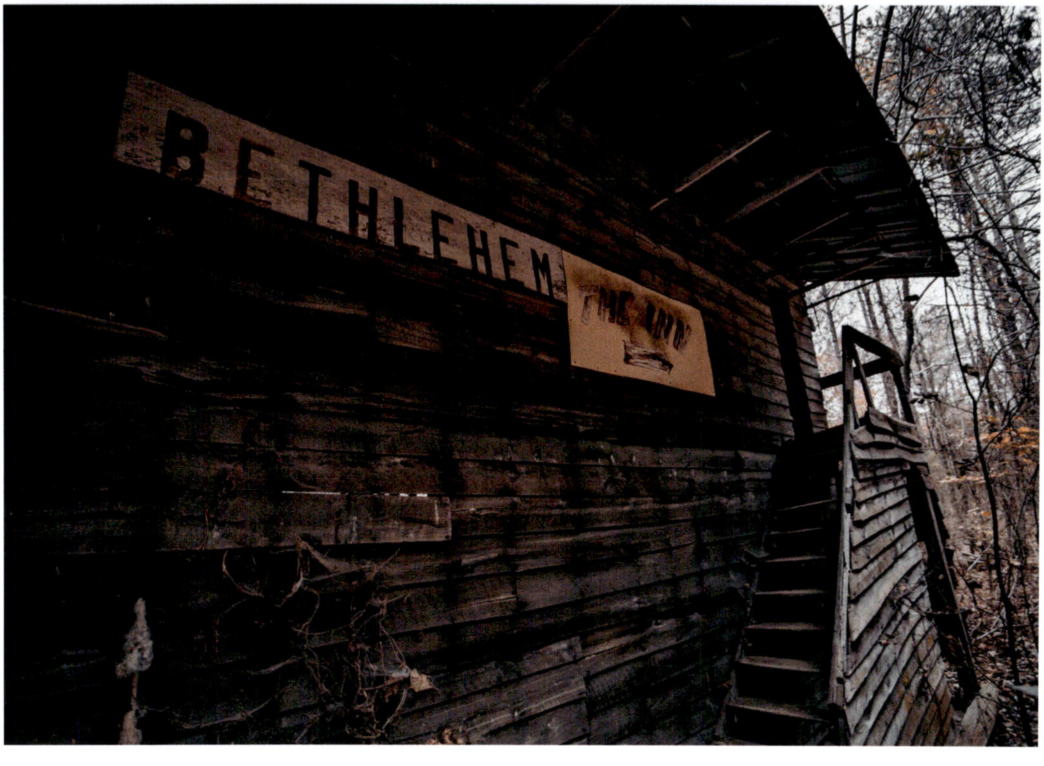

A sign on the back side of the nativity led guests to the next part of the show.

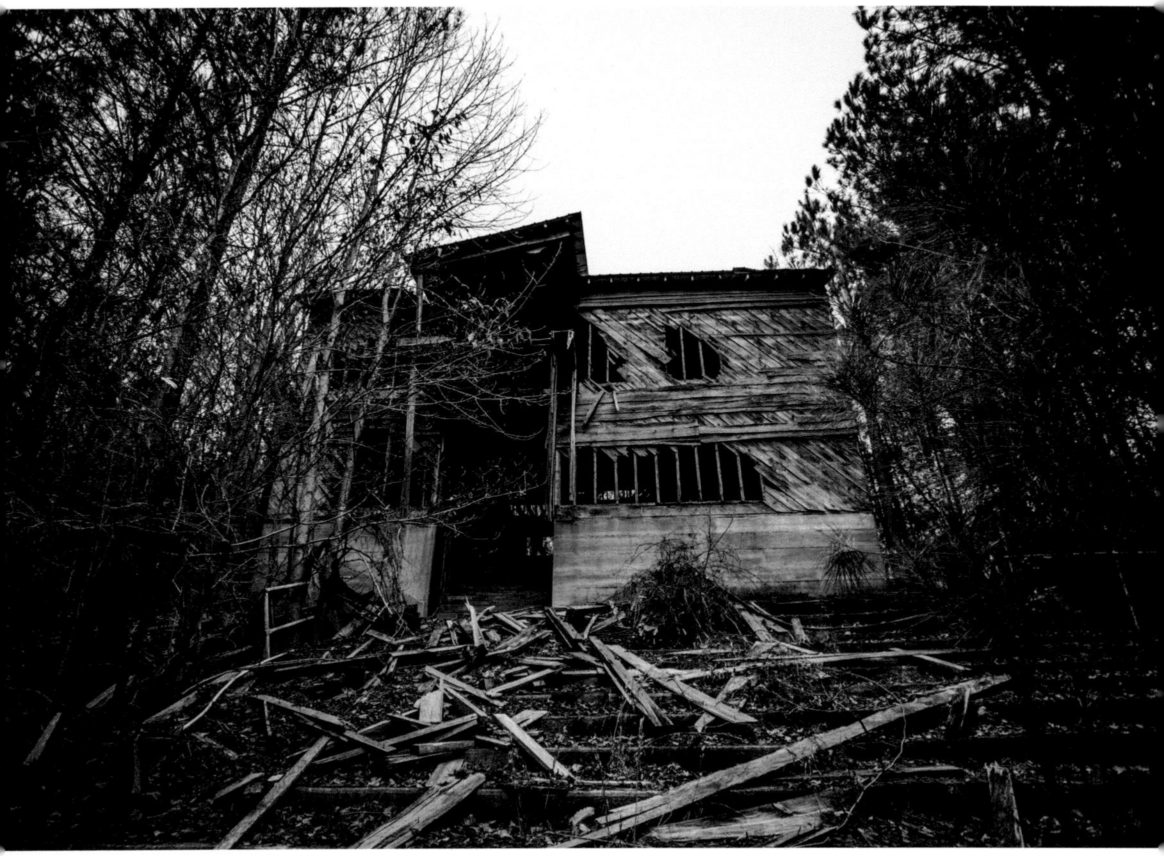

A view from the bottom of the amphitheater.

3

THE DIVORCE MANSION

I've noticed you can research a place for days, weeks, or months and never get ironclad evidence that what you have heard about something is factual, even if you have heard it from hundreds of people. This is the case for what has become known by locals as "the divorce mansion." This once beautiful home is probably the most modern abandoned home I have ever come across. According to the tax records, it was built in 1984. I want to reiterate that the stories I have read about this place are stories that were passed on to me by locals; I have been unable to confirm any of them.

People from the area tell a story of a family who had a beautiful life. A mom and a dad with two children decided to build this house. The land was owned by the mother's family and the father owned a construction business. They used the father's business and materials provided by him to build the house on the land the mother's family owned. According to locals, the marriage then began to struggle, and the parents soon decided to divorce. There was an intense legal battle over the property and its value so the ruling from the judge basically left the property in limbo forever.

Whether this story is really what happened is something that has eluded me but what I can tell you is that this beautiful home is now damaged beyond repair and becomes more engulfed by the landscape every day. I have personally watched the trees slowly grow tall enough to hide it from plain sight over the years since I have known about it. The house will one day slip completely behind the trees and brush trying so intently to conceal it. Will it be forgotten completely and become a mysterious speck in the forest on satellite imagery like so many other houses featured in this book?

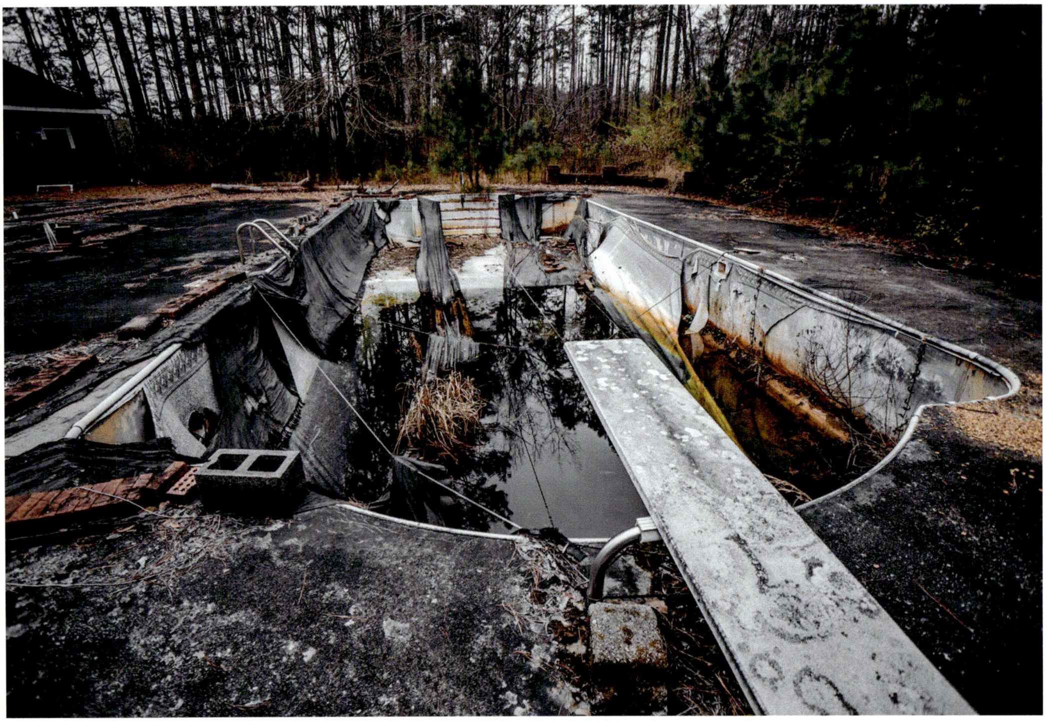

The swimming pool in the backyard damaged beyond repair.

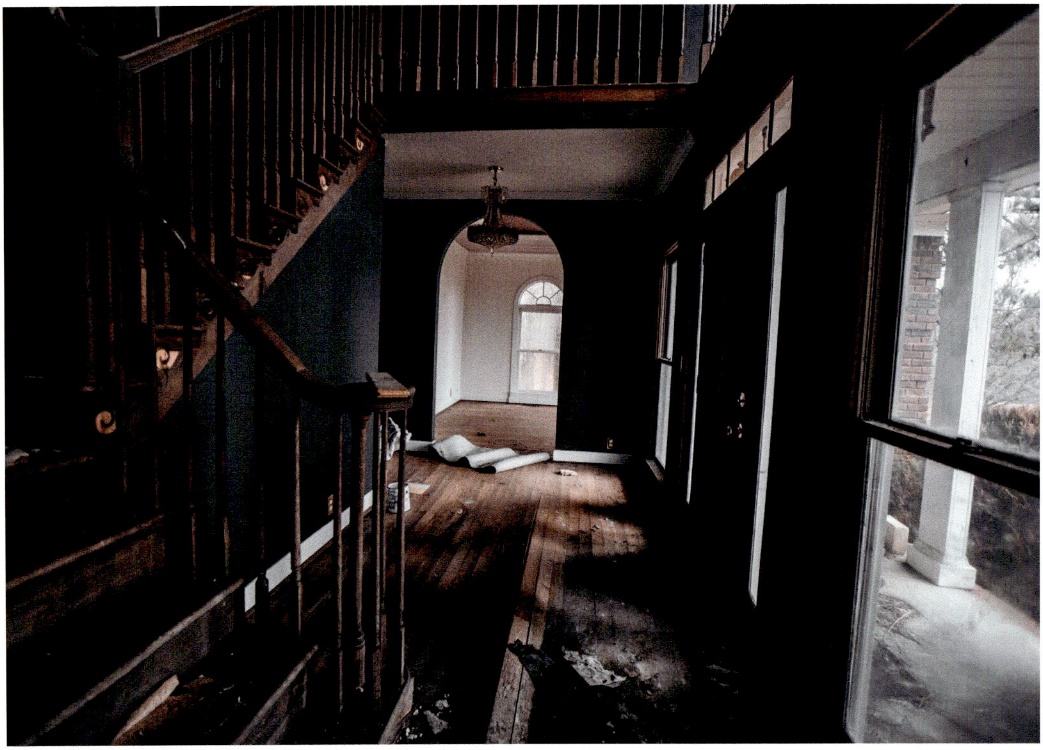

The worst natural damage is directly in front of both the front door and the back door.

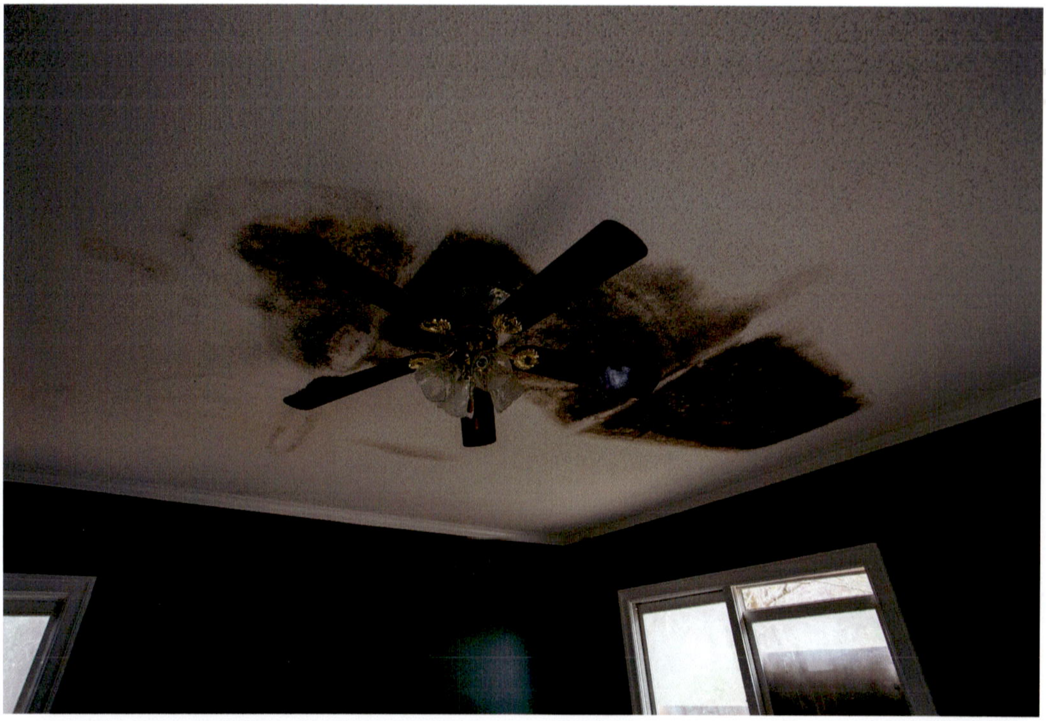

Black mold is starting to spread throughout the house. This large spot is found in a downstairs bedroom.

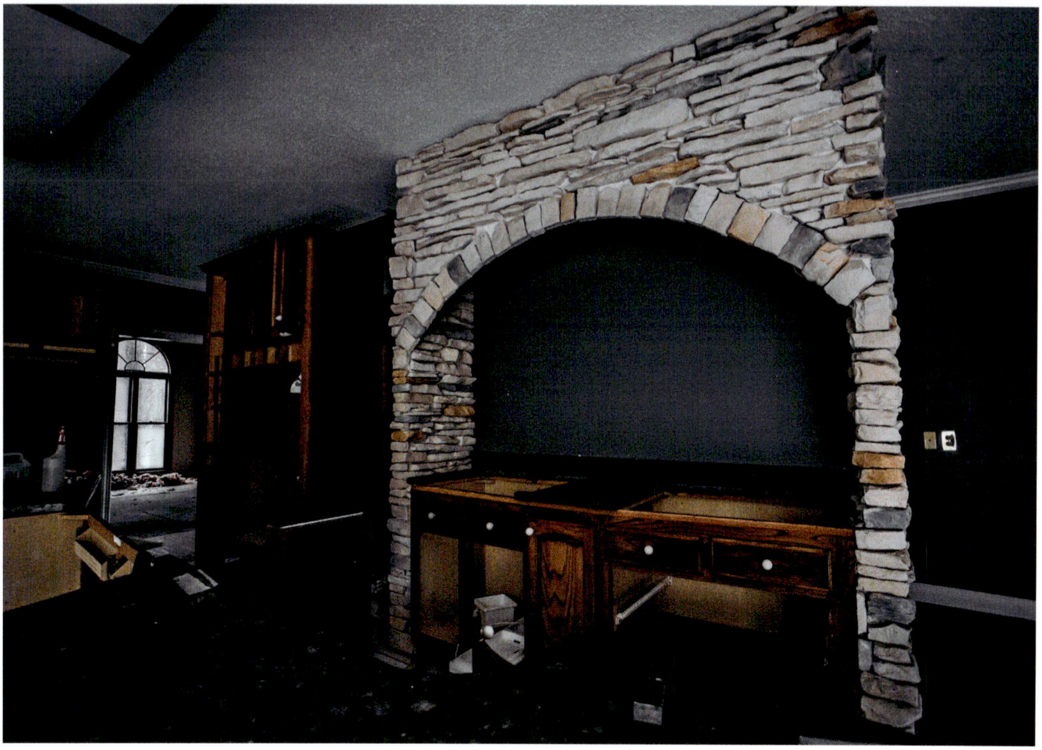

The stonework and woodwork in the kitchen are some of the most beautiful and intricate I have seen.

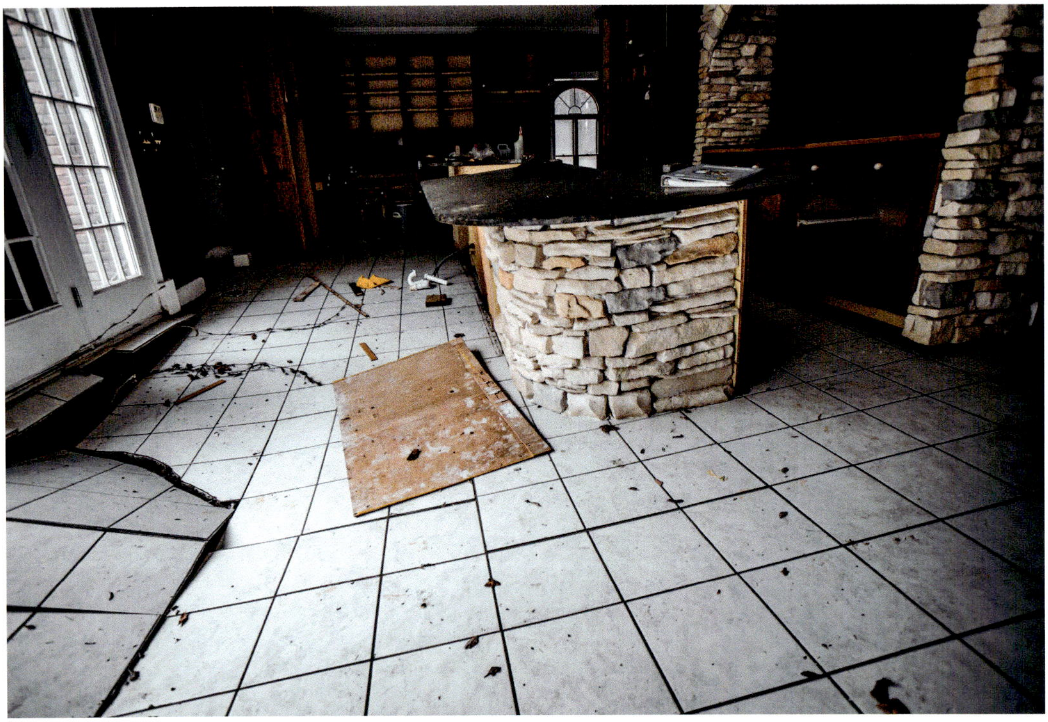

The floor has started to cave in front of the back door. It is unclear whether this was vandalism or a foundational issue.

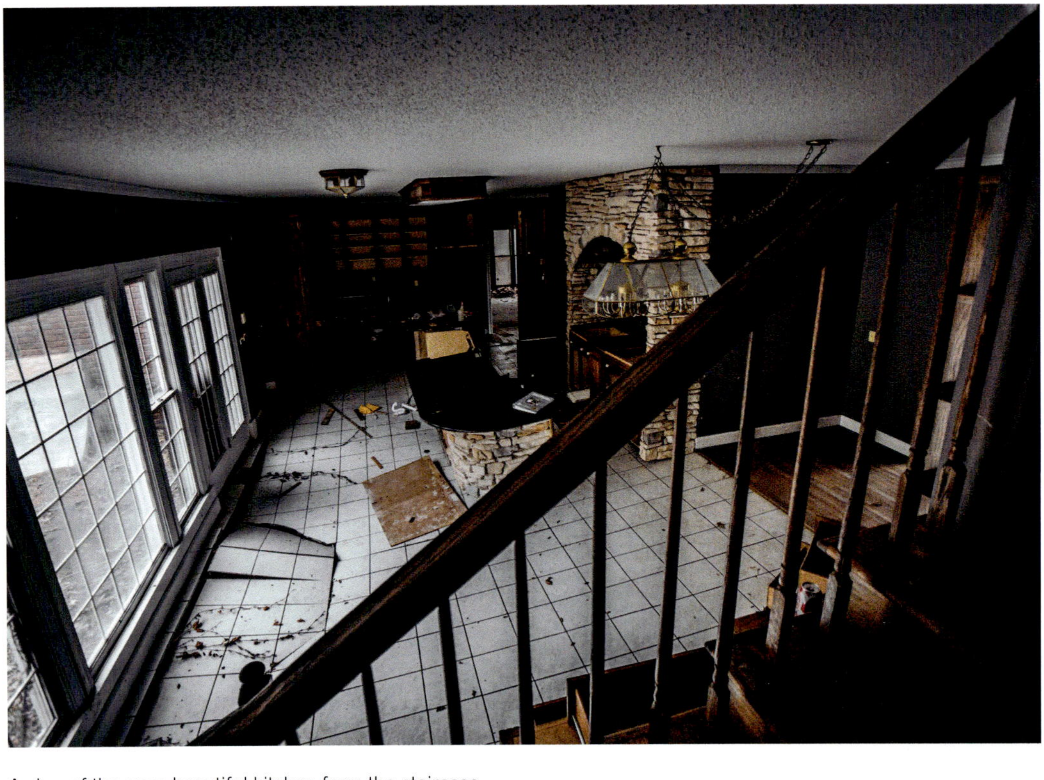

A view of the once beautiful kitchen from the staircase.

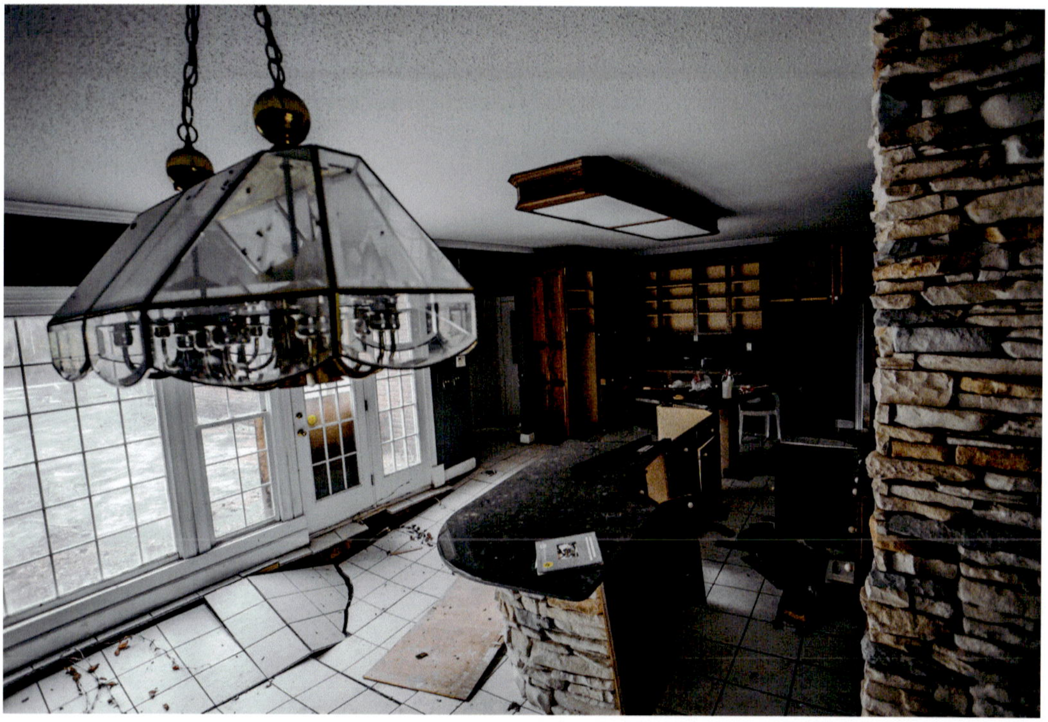

The lighting fixtures in the house have surprisingly not been taken.

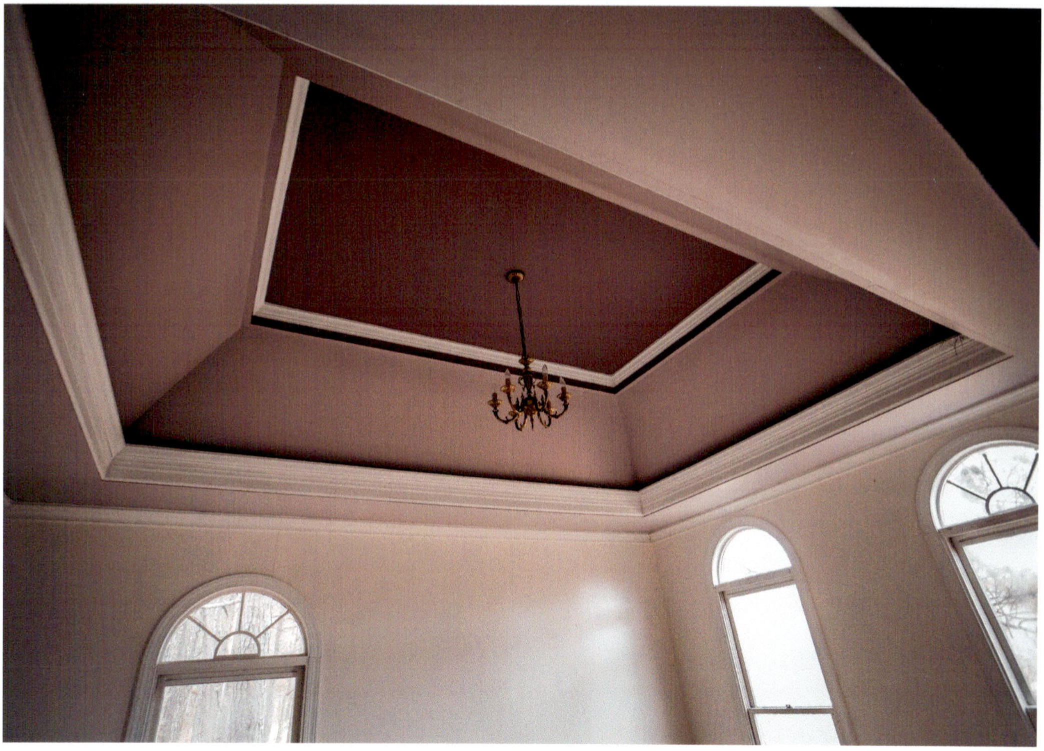

The vaulted ceilings in the home make the rooms feel particularly large and spacious.

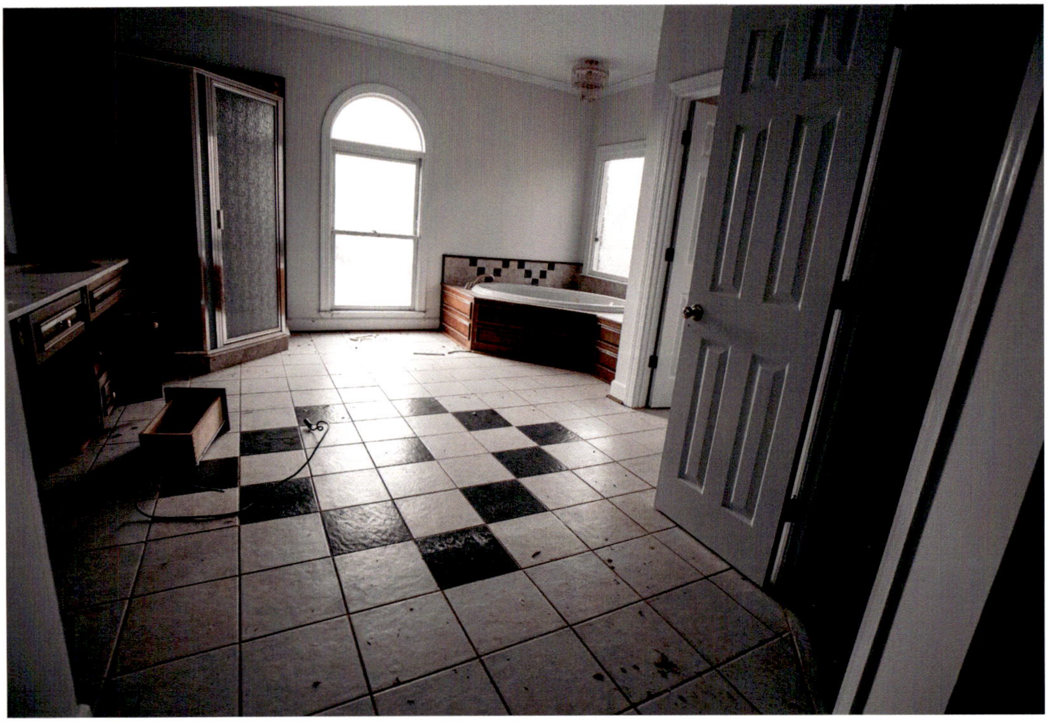

The modern bathroom features a jetted bath tub, large shower stall, and two walk-in closets.

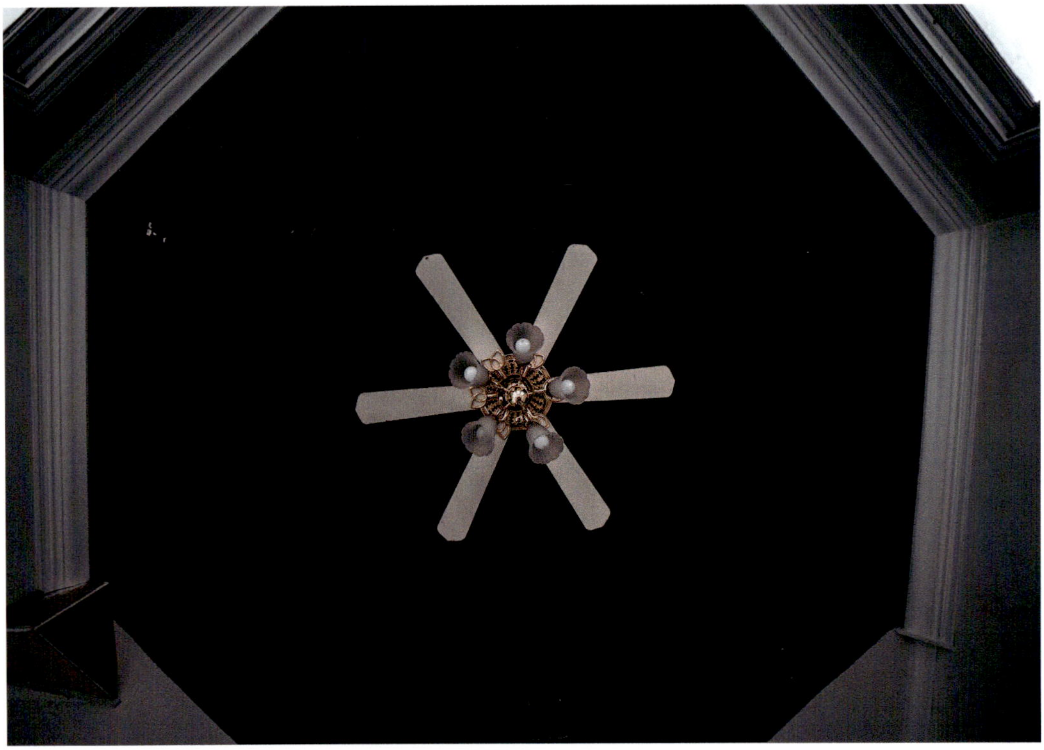

A view of the vaulted ceiling and a ceiling fan in one of the bedrooms.

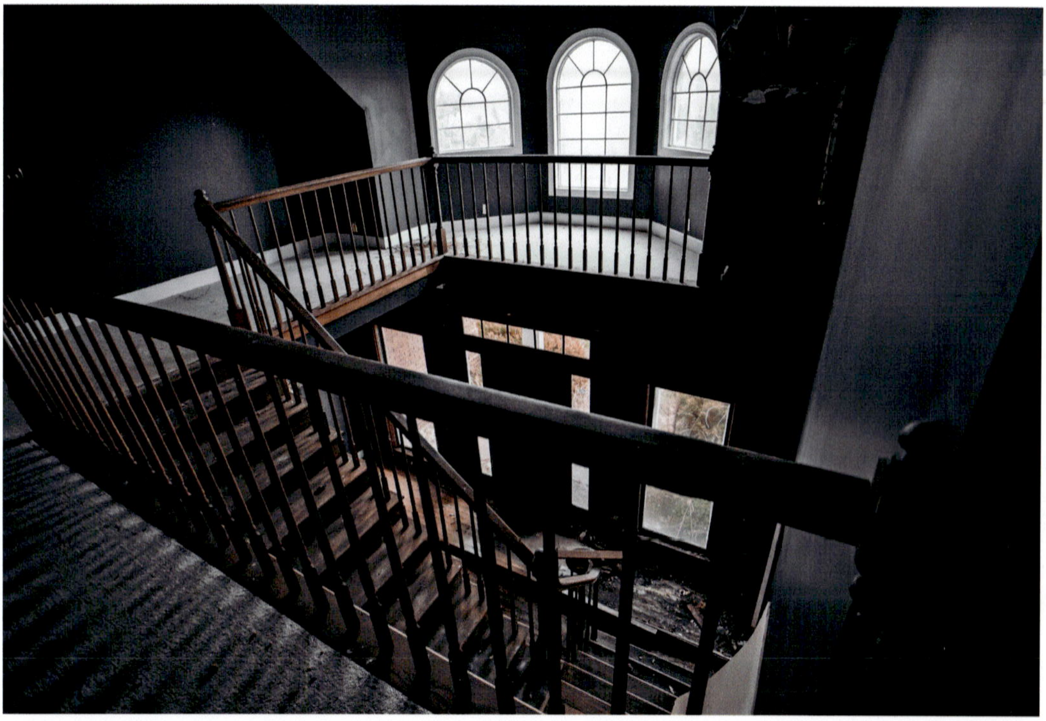

This overhead view of the staircase at the entrance of the residence shows the intricacy of the architecture.

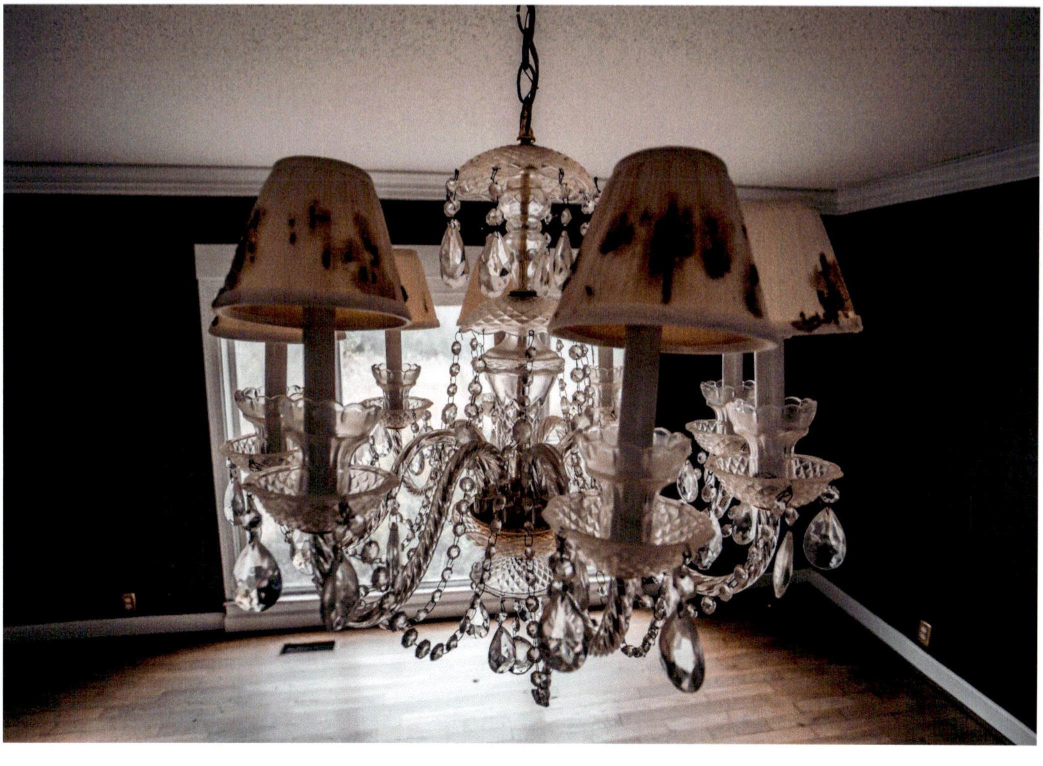

A beautiful chandelier left behind.

4

THE DECLINE OF MENTAL HEALTH

I drive up a long, paved road that leads to a set of buildings to find one with a large number of cars parked behind it. This heavy traffic would normally deter explorers such as myself but approximately 100 yards from this building is a four-story structure with boards on every entrance and window. The building itself looks like something you would see on a television show about the zombie apocalypse. If this were a zombie movie, I have definitely just arrived at ground zero, where the first zombies started taking bites out of the hospital staff. We drive around the building multiple times, more than likely drawing attention to ourselves, but we had to find a safe place to ditch the car. We finally settle on a spot just behind a water tower between the two buildings. Immediately we notice cameras pointing in every direction on the busy building, then a sign letting us know that we are trying to explore an abandoned structure right next to a 911 call center and across the street from a state trooper office.

We grab our camera gear and start our trek to the back of the building in hopes of finding a way in. The next sign that might deter most explorers: "US Military Operations, Do Not Enter" hangs sideways off of a metal gate. Despite the sign, it appears as if it has been years since anyone has stepped foot on the property so we decide to continue on. Admittedly, this was not the best decision.

We locate an open door on the back of the hospital and start to explore. Once we are about halfway through the mostly empty building, we notice that the power is on in at least one wing of the old hospital. This is rare but occasionally for whatever reason these abandoned places still have electricity. We continue to walk through until we start noticing a repetitive noise. We do not realize how loud the sound actually is until we finally start getting closer to the source, a fire alarm. We panic thinking this alarm was triggered by us. We leave and decide to come back another time.

A few days go by and we decide to go back and try our luck but first we walk the perimeter of the building and notice that the alarm is still going off. We finish our exploration of the building and decide to start digging into the history of it. This was a pretty recently closed hospital with a huge sign displaying "North Alabama Regional Hospital" on the front of the building so the history was not hard to find. The hospital itself was only opened for thirty-eight years as a psychiatric hospital but previously it was a tuberculosis sanitorium. A quick search on social media for it revealed countless stories from people who worked there talking about how scary it was even before it closed, with many claiming to have seen ghosts and hear things while working night shifts.

Its closure in 2015 was part of a controversial move by Alabama government cutting the spending on mental health throughout the state. North Alabama Regional Hospital employed 149 people at the time of its closing and housed forty-one patients. At the time of its closure, it left Alabama with only one psychiatric hospital throughout the entire state.

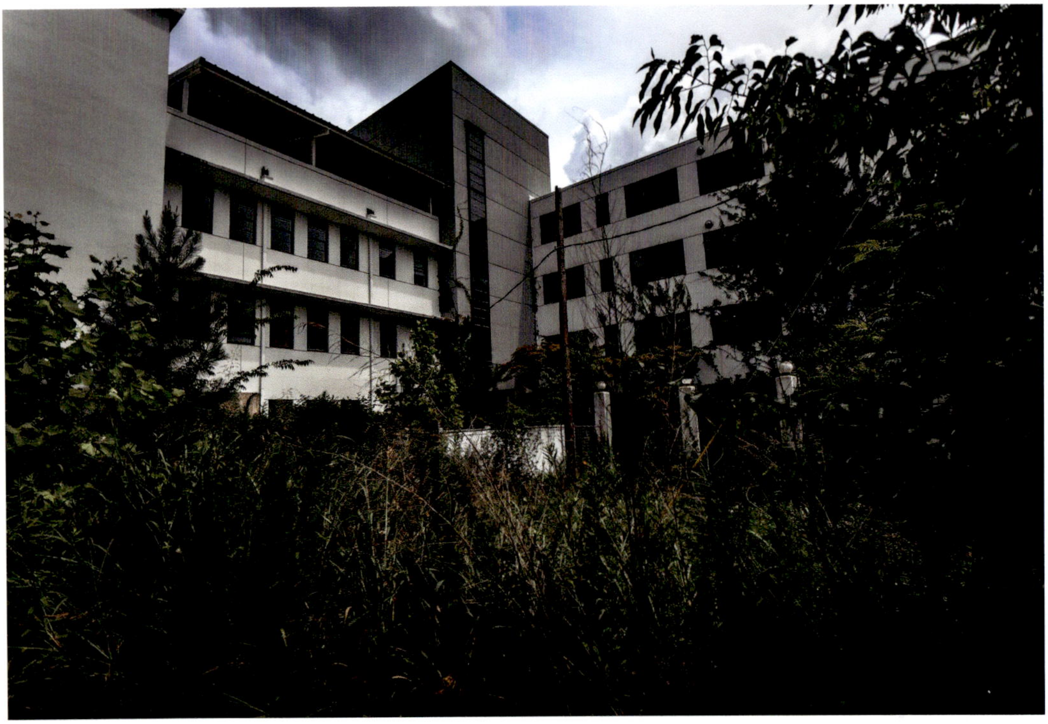

The exterior of the hospital looks post-apocalyptic.

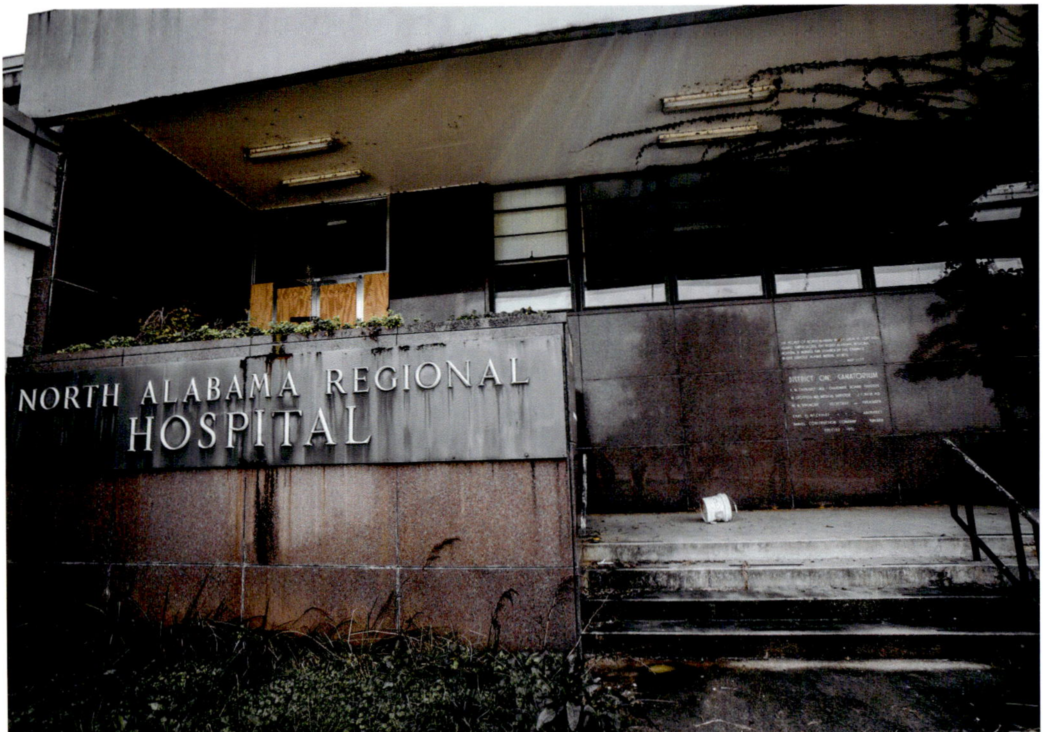

A sign from when the building was a functional hospital.

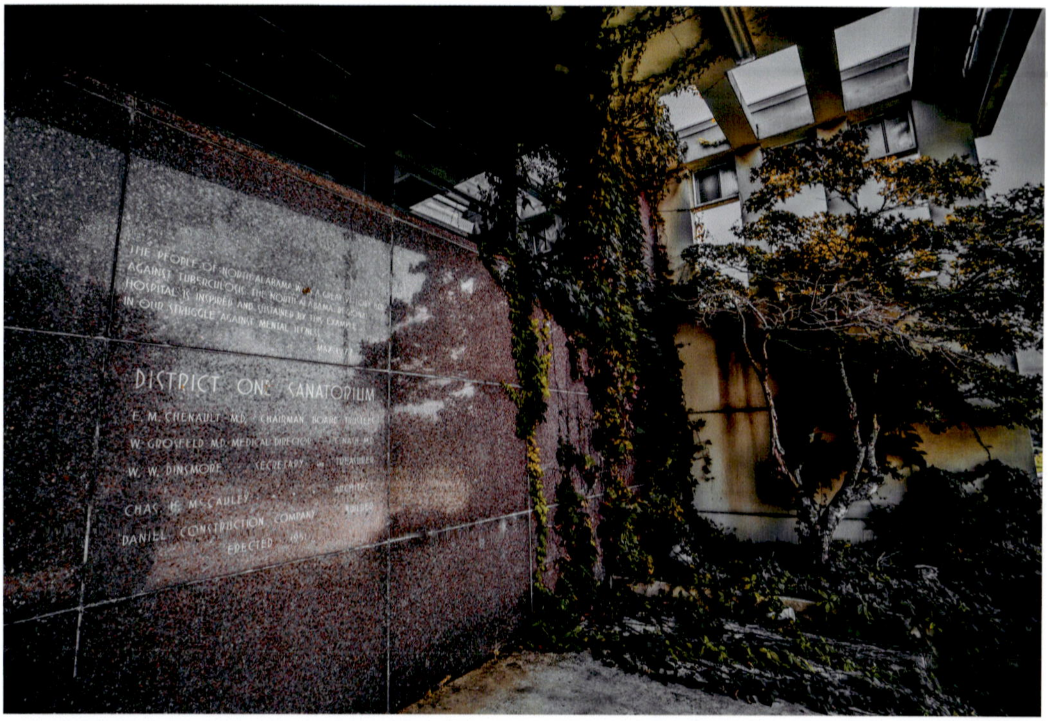

The sign for the sanitorium is still present but is almost covered by vines.

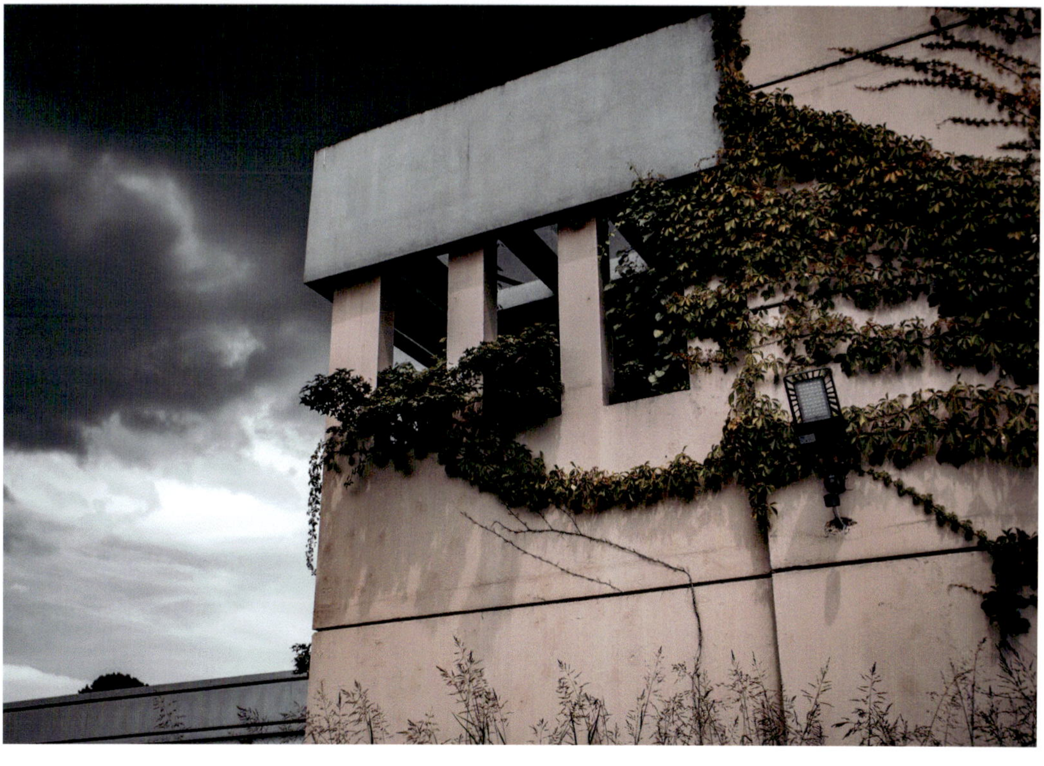

Vines have found their way into the break areas on the top floor.

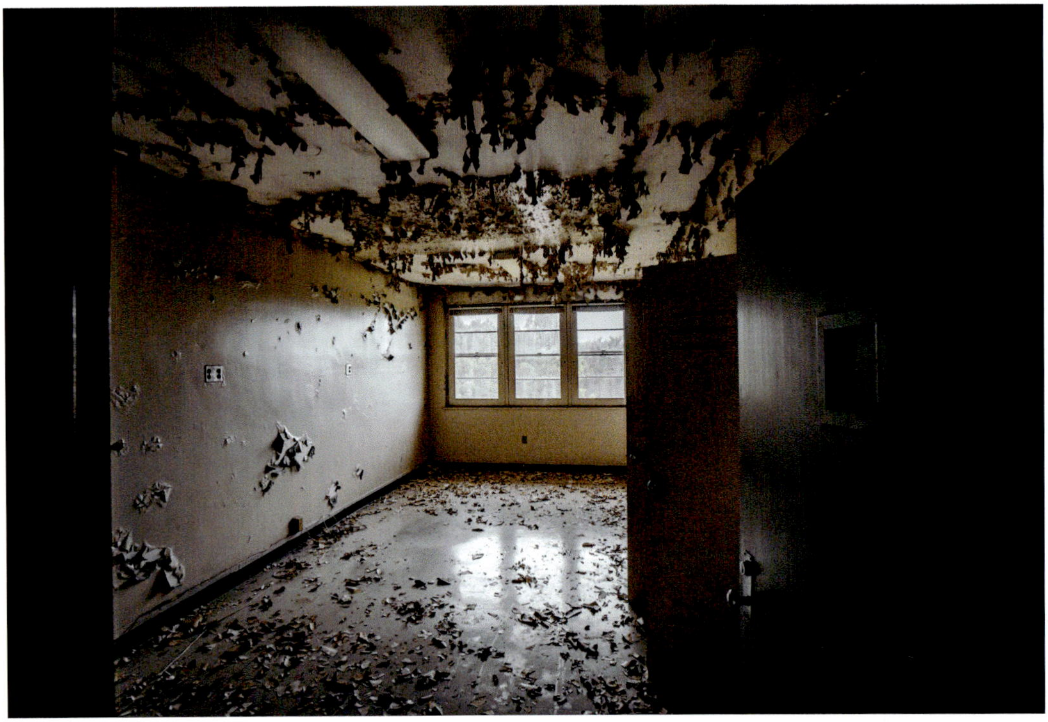

A room with the paint chipping off the ceiling due to age and temperature exposure.

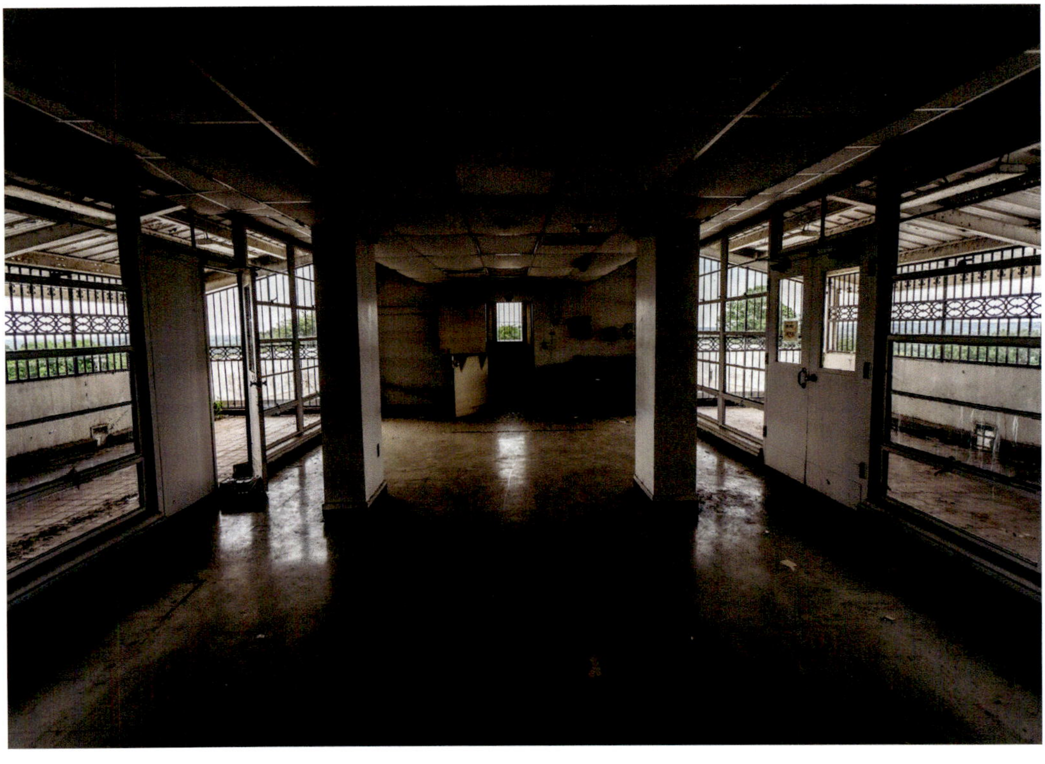

A break room on the top floor gives a view in all directions.

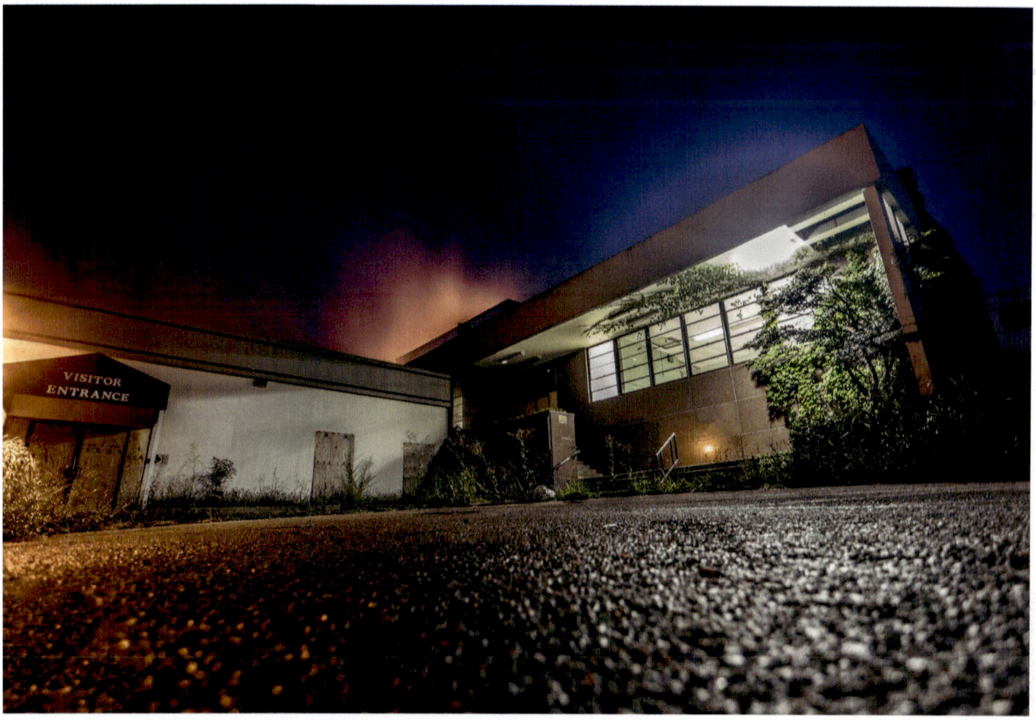

The hospital having electricity gives an eerie feeling at night.

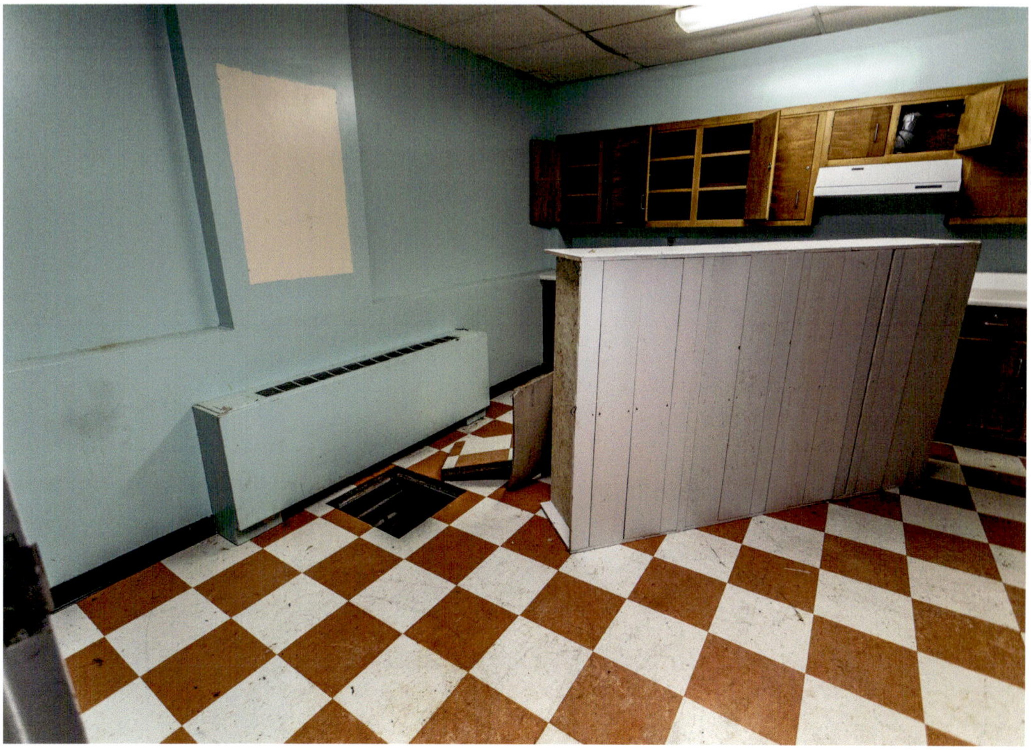

A checkerboard floor in one of the rooms.

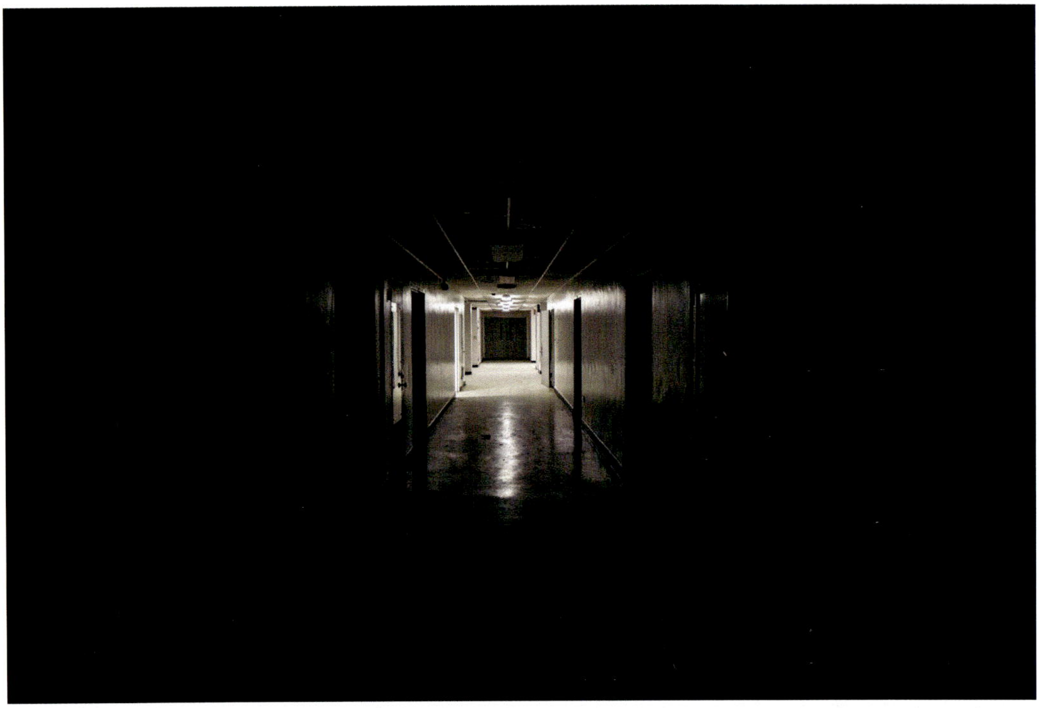

A hallway where the power is still working on one side.

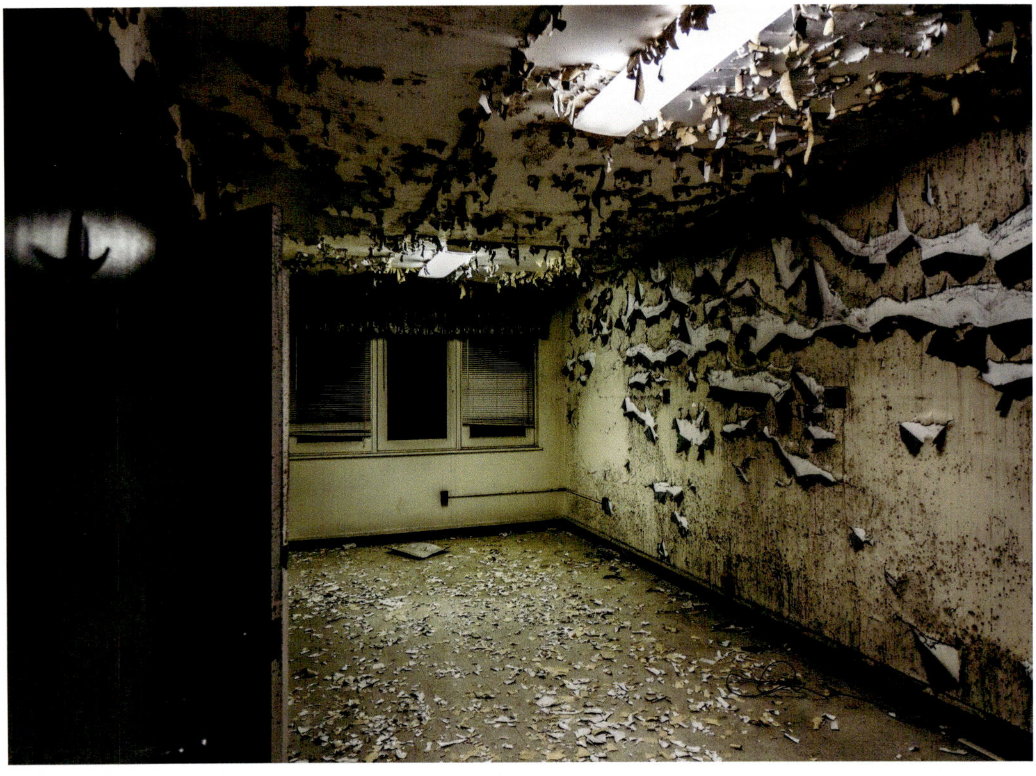

The rooms with paint chipping away feel even more sinister at night.

5

THE SCHOOLS

I will never step foot into an abandoned school without immediately being transported back to when I walked similar halls. I often fool myself into smelling the same things. My memory often recalls vividly the scent of chalk dust, pencil shavings, or the strange combination of pizza and corn that schools tended to serve. I have come across several schools on this journey, and I decided to include them all in the same chapter because the details are always so similar.

A huge problem I have encountered is that when schools are abandoned, the word travels fast and it never takes long before vandals break windows or cover the walls with graffiti. I discovered that it is even more rare that items are left behind because usually a closure is just a relocation. Teachers often have plenty of time to transfer their items to the new buildings.

Older schools almost always have hardwood floors throughout the entire building that give way to water damage easily. The first school I have included was built in the late 1930s and is a series of hardwood hallways in a U-shaped building. Damage to the hardwood makes every step questionable. The gymnasium settled in the middle of building has corners collapsing but the center of the basketball court is still in relatively good shape. Behind the goal on the far end is a curtained stage with a piano. I tried to explore the backstage area but found the floor to be too risky. Only fourteen years since the last class graduated from here, this old school did not age well.

The gymnasium certainly grabs your attention with the bleachers waiting eternally for a crowd that will never come. The halls still bear pictures reminding the students to walk quietly and not to chew gum. The highlight of this explore for me is the science lab. The desks are all removed from this room, but in the front of the room rests an island with microscopes, a few Bunsen burners, and a sink. I walk past this island and find a closet filled from floor to ceiling with shelves of chemicals and lab equipment.

The next school I have included was a little tougher to research as sections of the campus were used for Head Start programs and other education related offices. The condition of it was much worse than the significantly older school previously mentioned. The ceiling in the center of the school was completely collapsed and water flowed into the hallways. It is hard to tell what was naturally falling apart and what vandals had done. The gymnasium here had a newer hardwood floor, but the damage seemed much worse. Instead of rotting, the gym floor buckled and raised up off the foundation in rows. Every step I took, the floor creaked and popped.

The playground shrouded in small pine trees is almost completely hidden. The classrooms once graced by countless children were almost completely desolate save the occasional desk or the one room that housed hundreds of trophies. This struck me. I thought about how proudly my high school displayed its trophies and wondered what those athletes and scholars would think about seeing the token of their hard work covered in cobwebs and dust in a building almost ready to collapse in on itself. I thought about the ones who probably now tell stories to their kids about how they were the victors. The sweat, blood, and tears that were probably shed over some of the accomplishments and the prize are forgotten. Perhaps this is a lesson. Maybe some stories will never die, regardless of mold, water damage, or a building losing its structural integrity. The prize truly is the story and not the shiny thing you are handed when you are done.

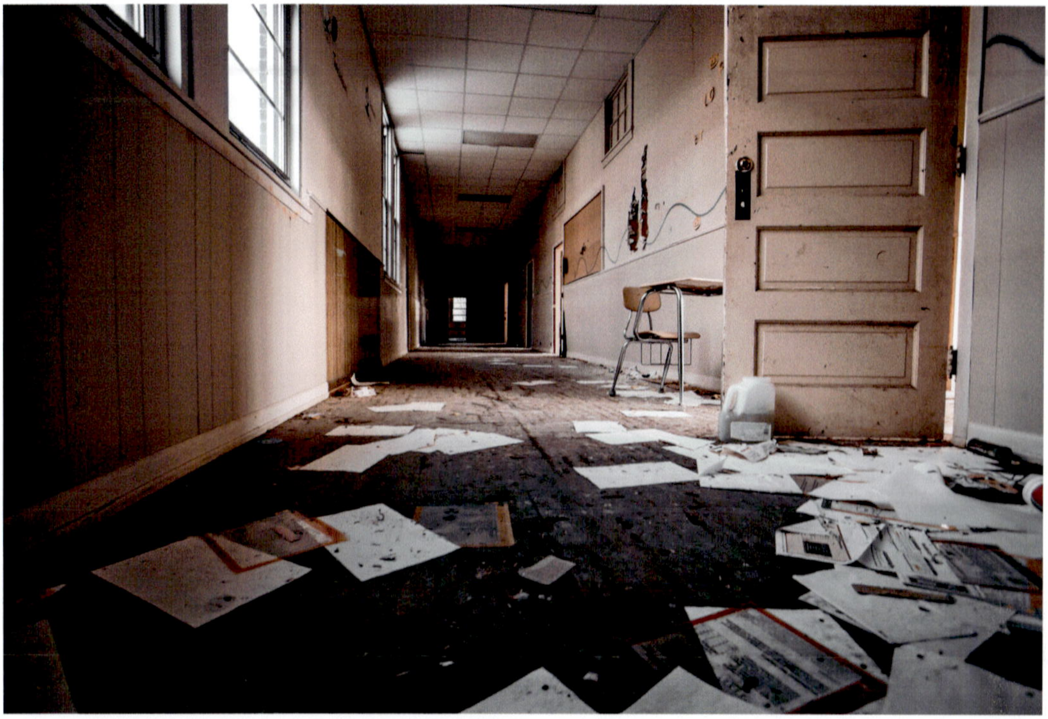

A lonely desk sits in the hallway outside the classroom.

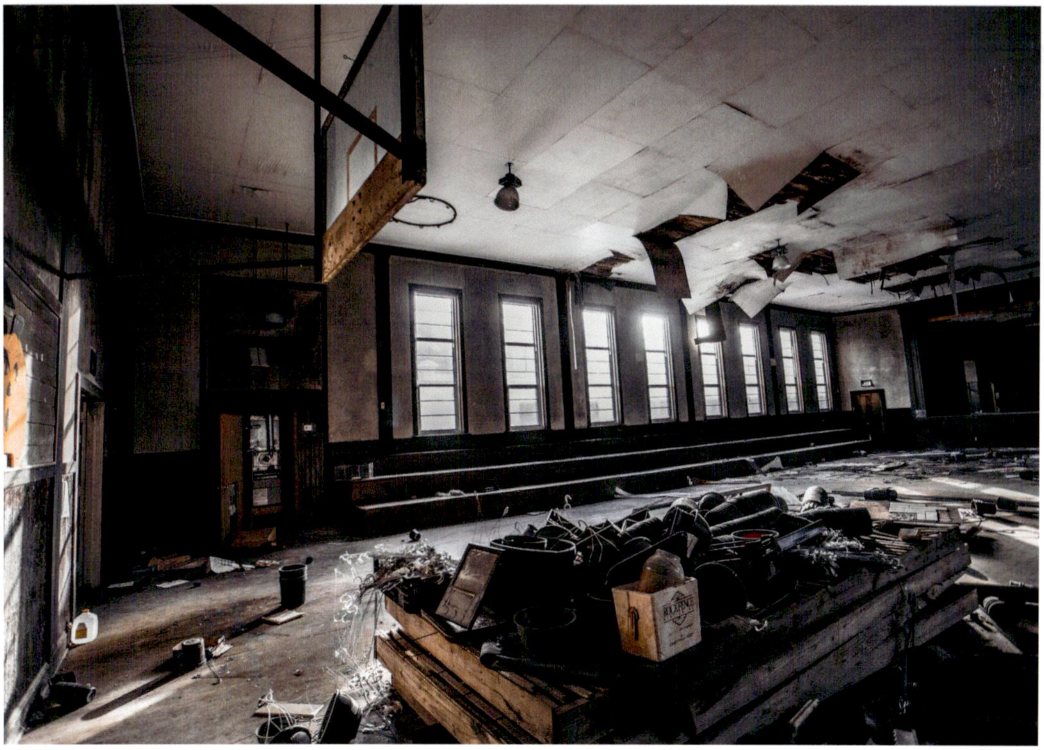

The old gym is starting to show severe signs of decay but has been used for some events since the school's closure.

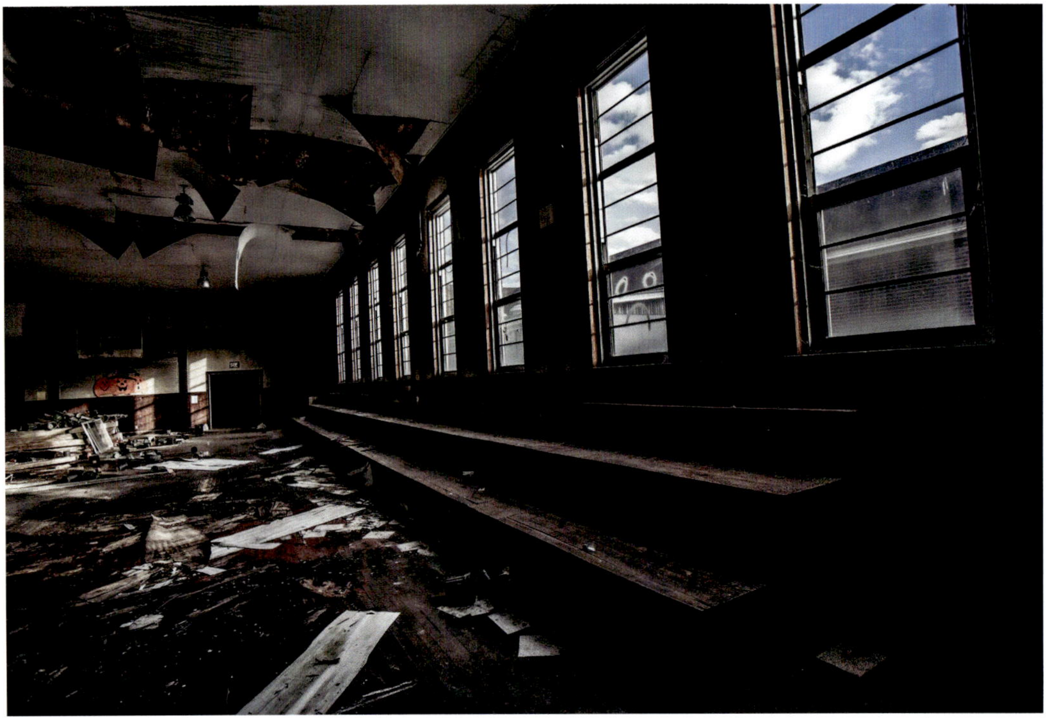

The old bleachers provided us a safe path where the floor was too soft to walk.

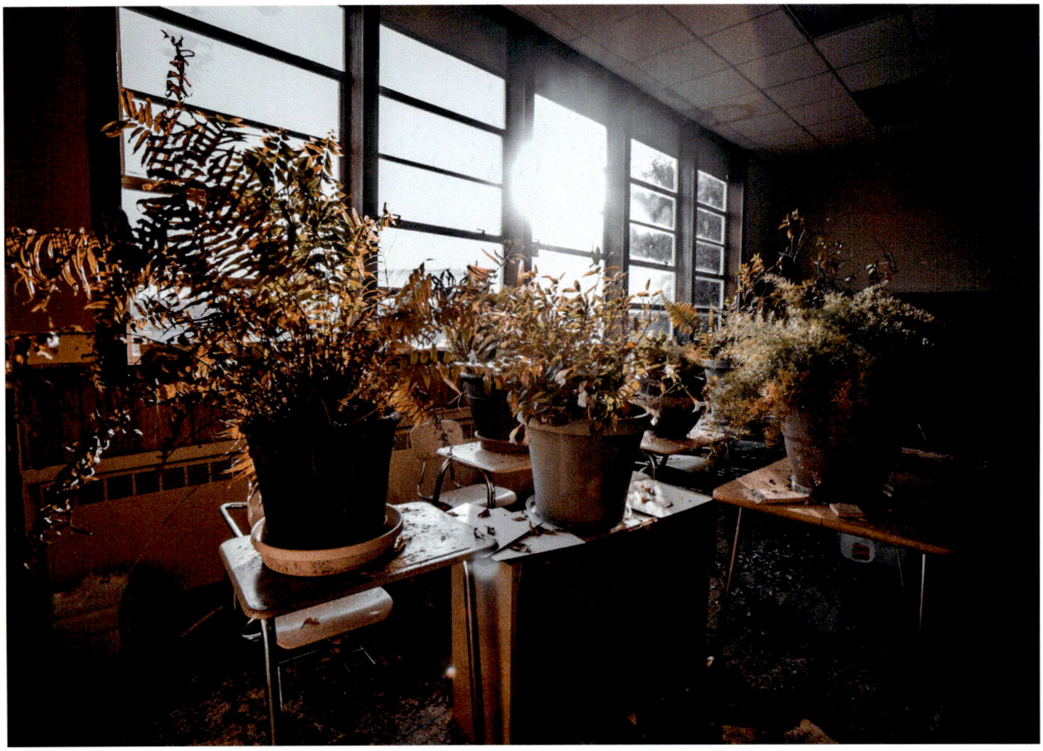

Plants in a classroom still trying to survive.

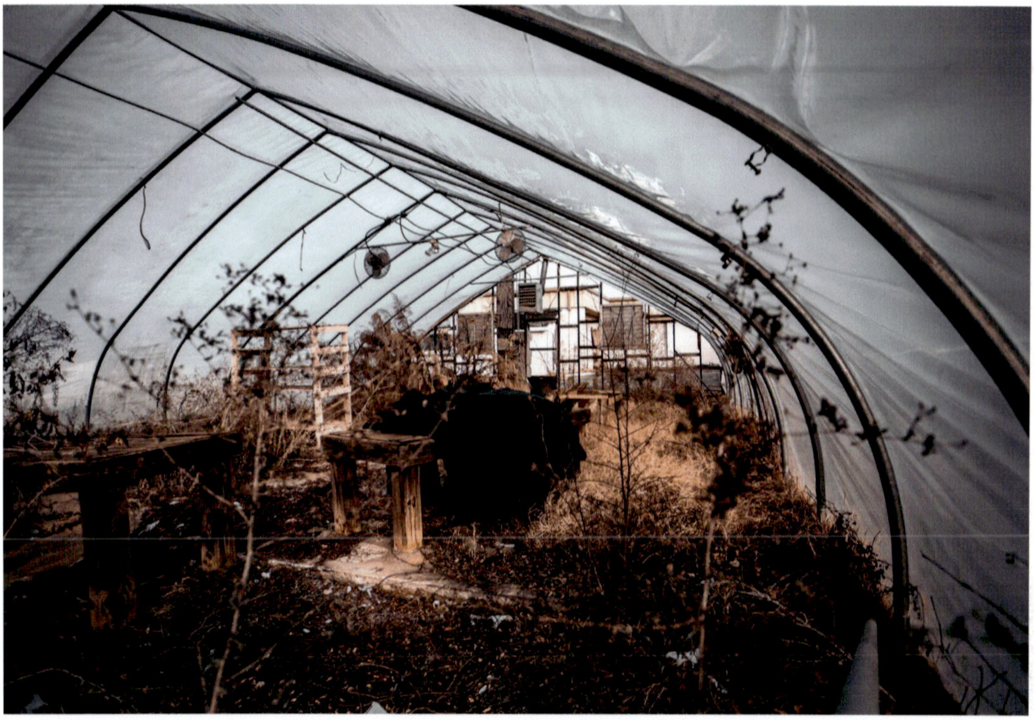

The old greenhouse provides the plants enough shelter from direct sunlight but water cannot reach them.

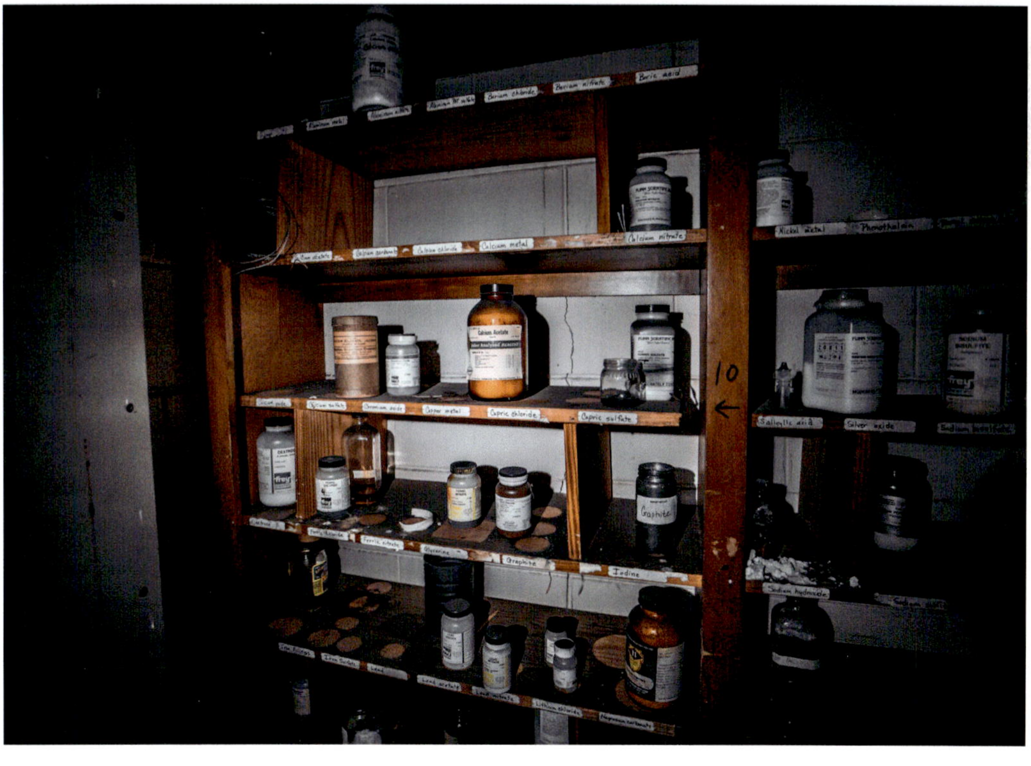

The old science lab still fully stocked with chemicals.

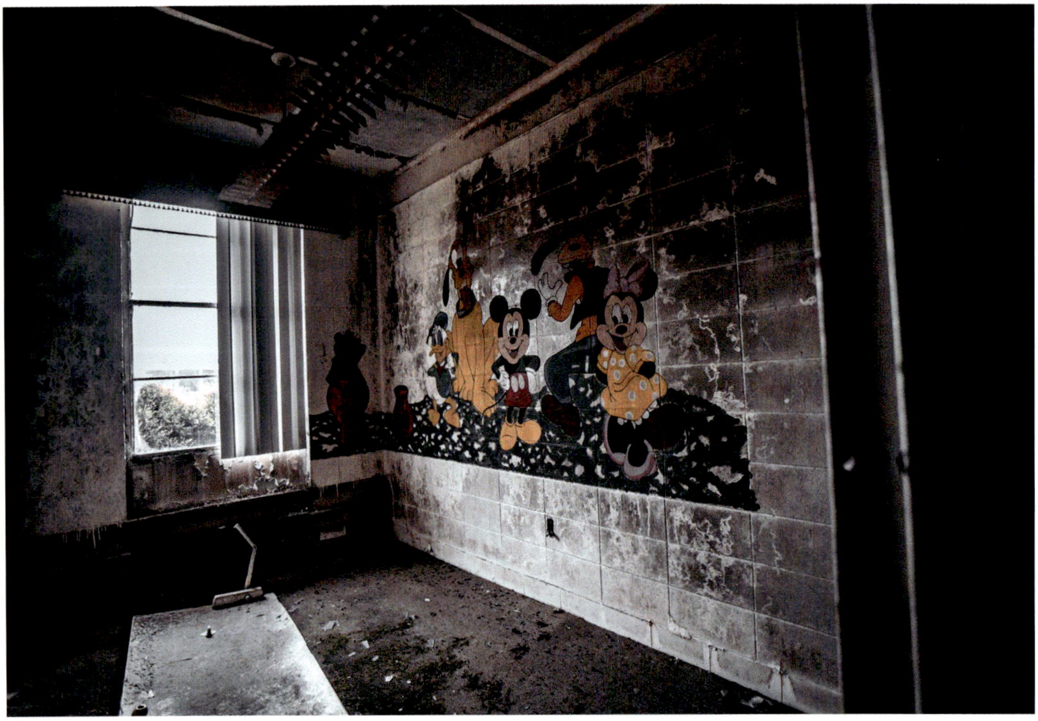

A mural in the school from when it was a Head Start program.

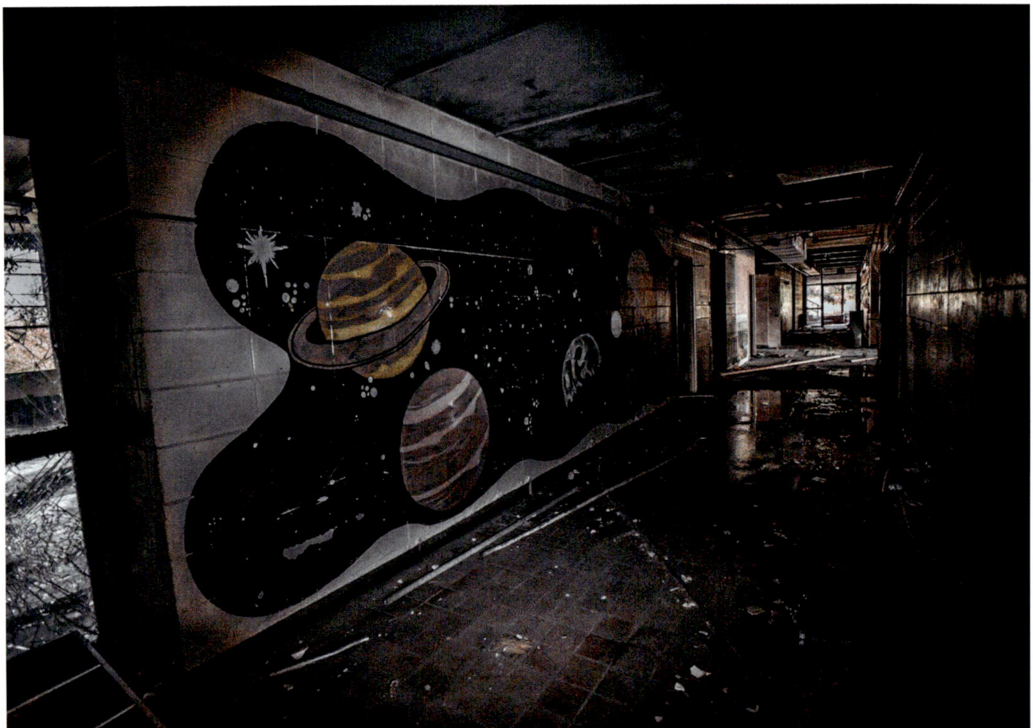

A space mural on the main hallway.

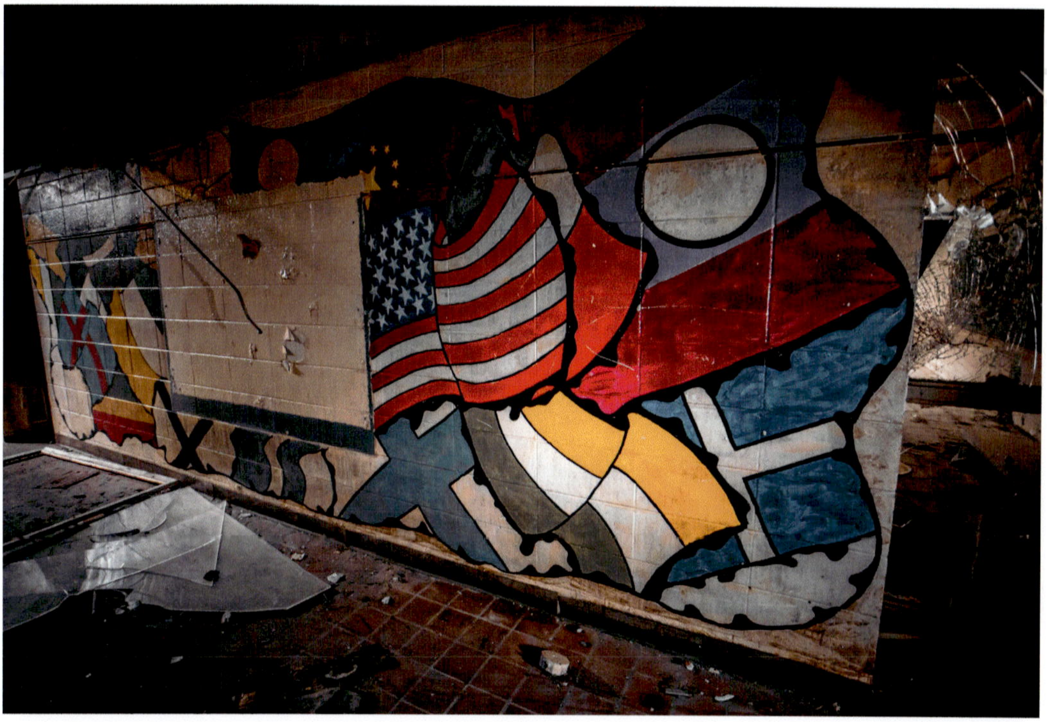

Another mural showing the flags of different countries.

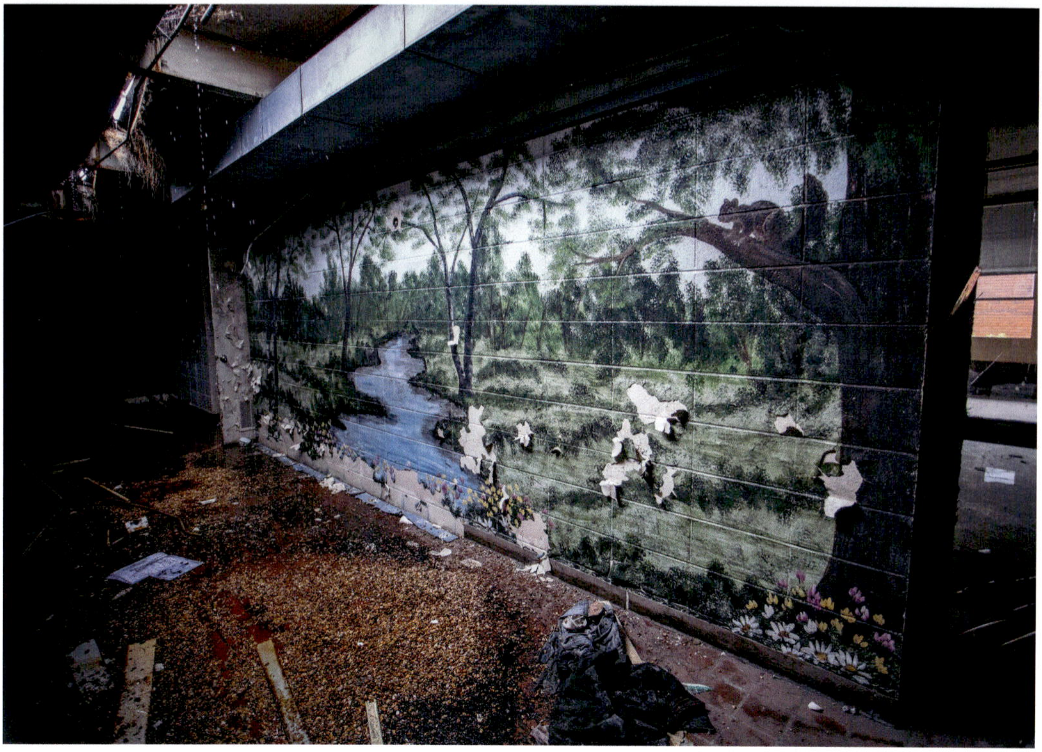

Water drips from the ceiling and collects on the ground in the main corridor leading to the library.

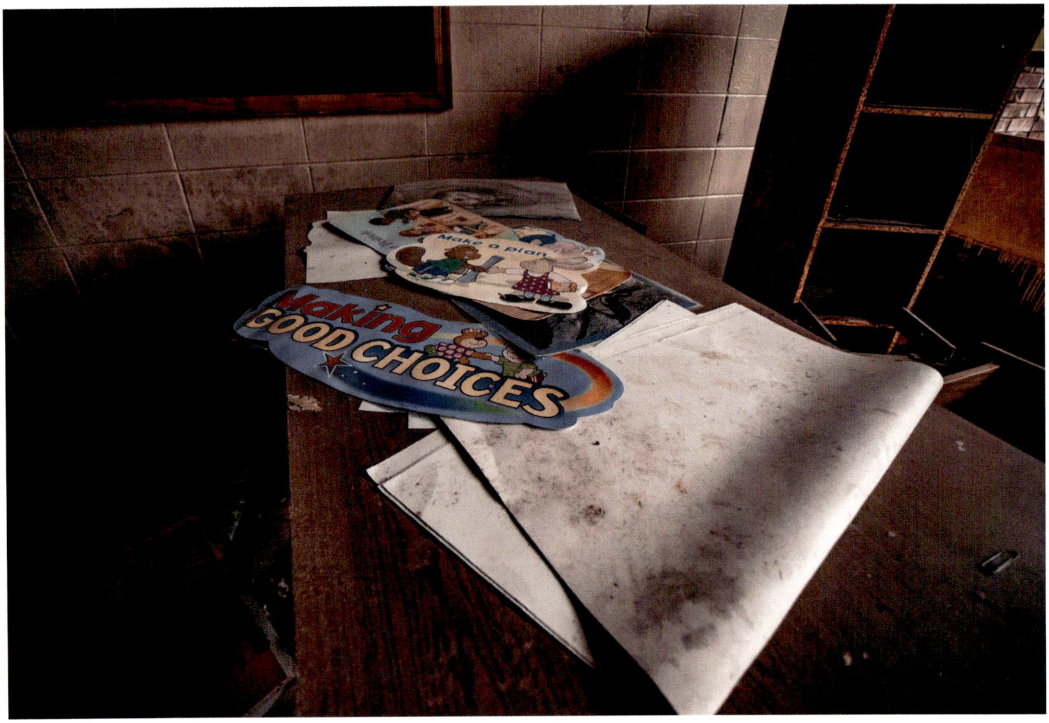

Classroom decorations teaching the children to focus on their decision-making skills still sits on a desk in this old classroom.

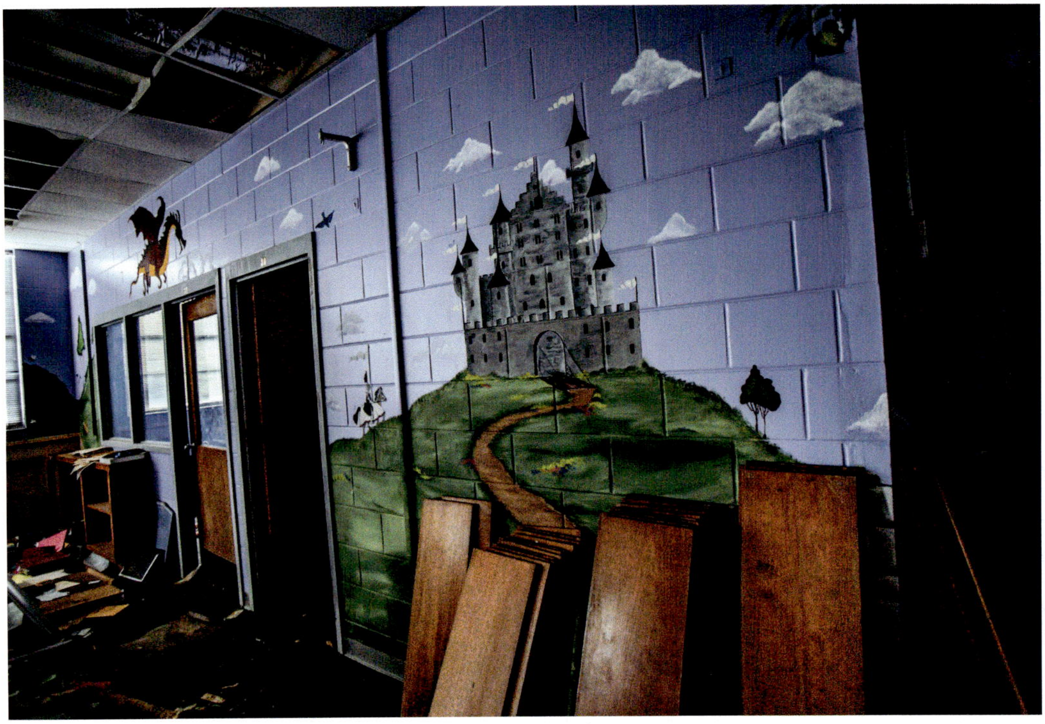

A mural in the library.

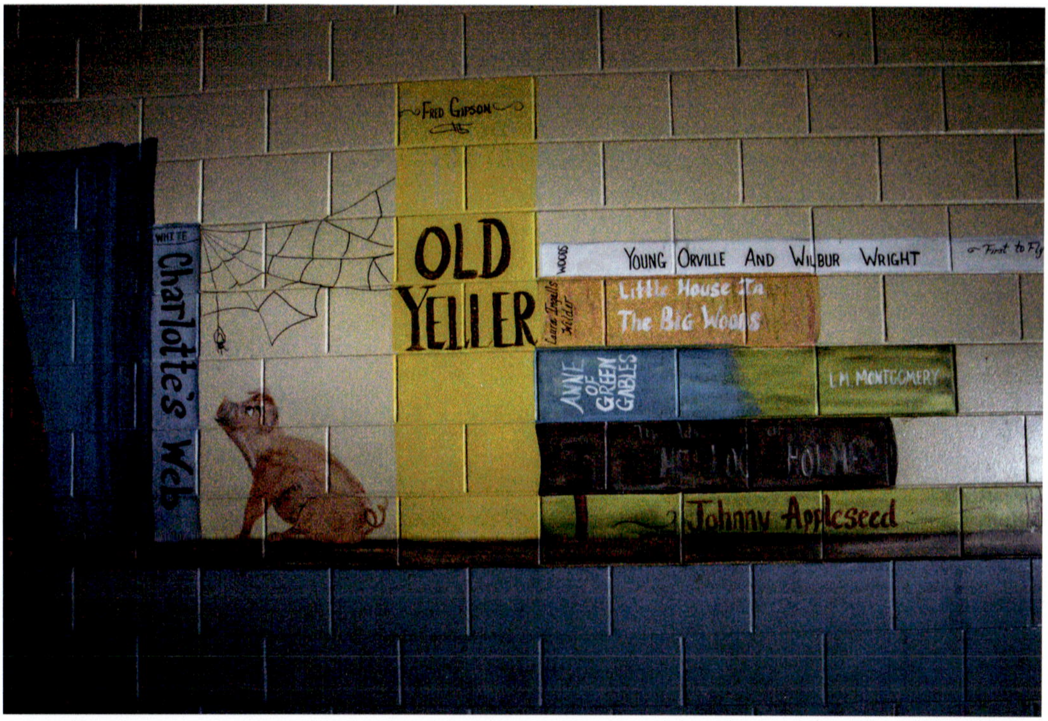

This mural on a main hallway pays homage to classic books.

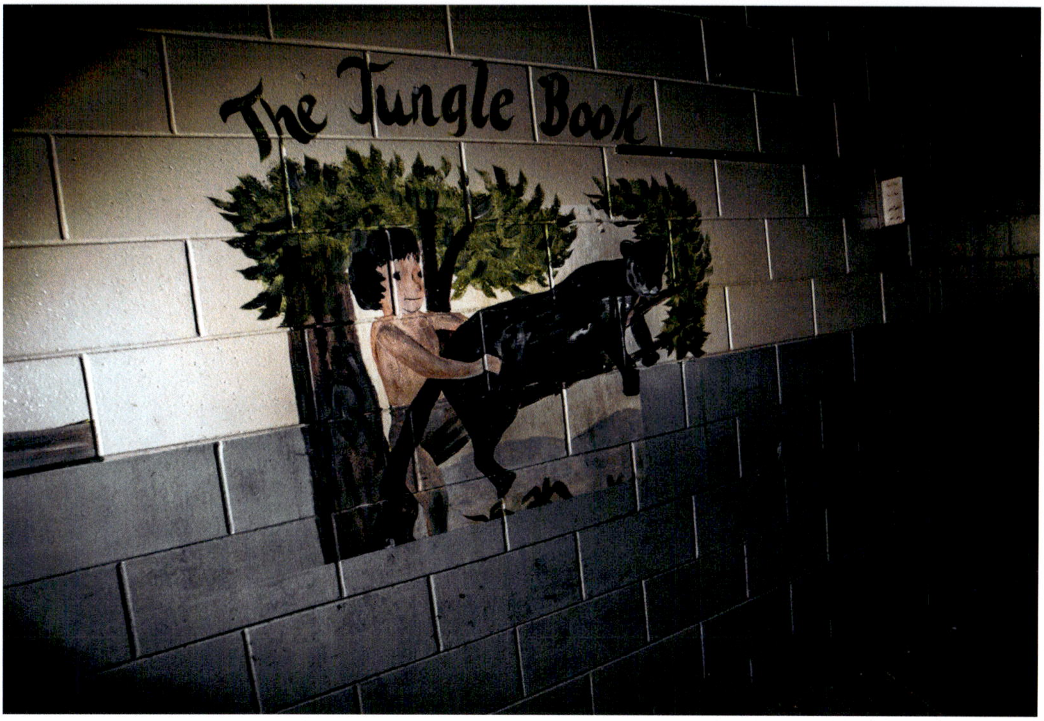

Just across from the book mural another kid favorite, *The Jungle Book*, gets its own mural.

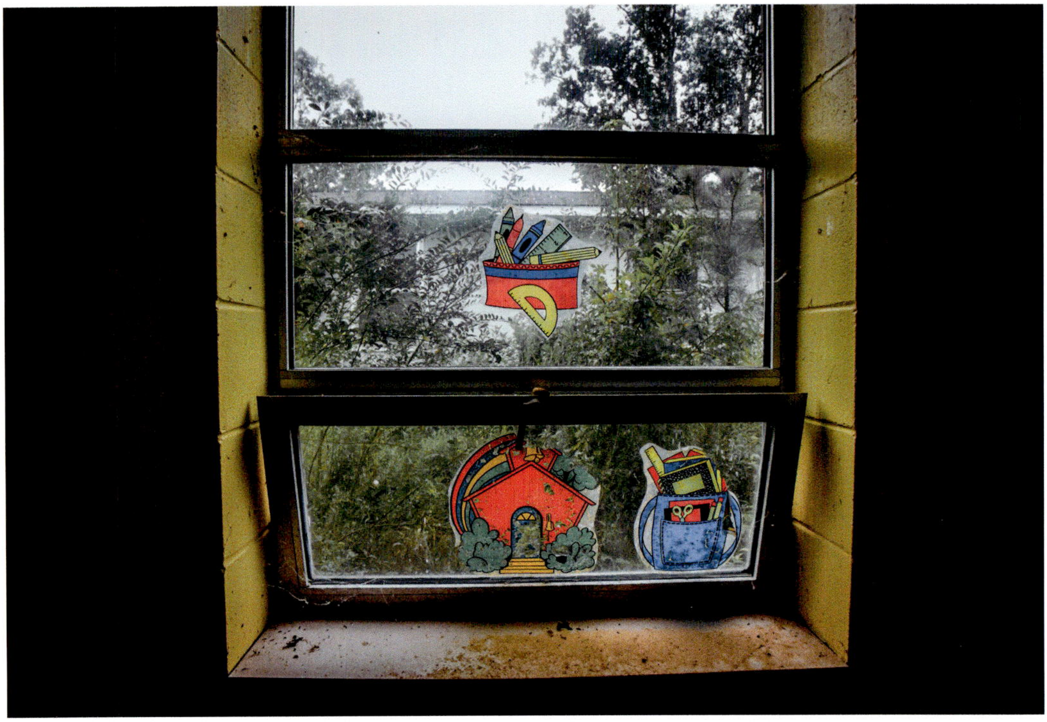

Window clings still adorn a few of the classroom windows.

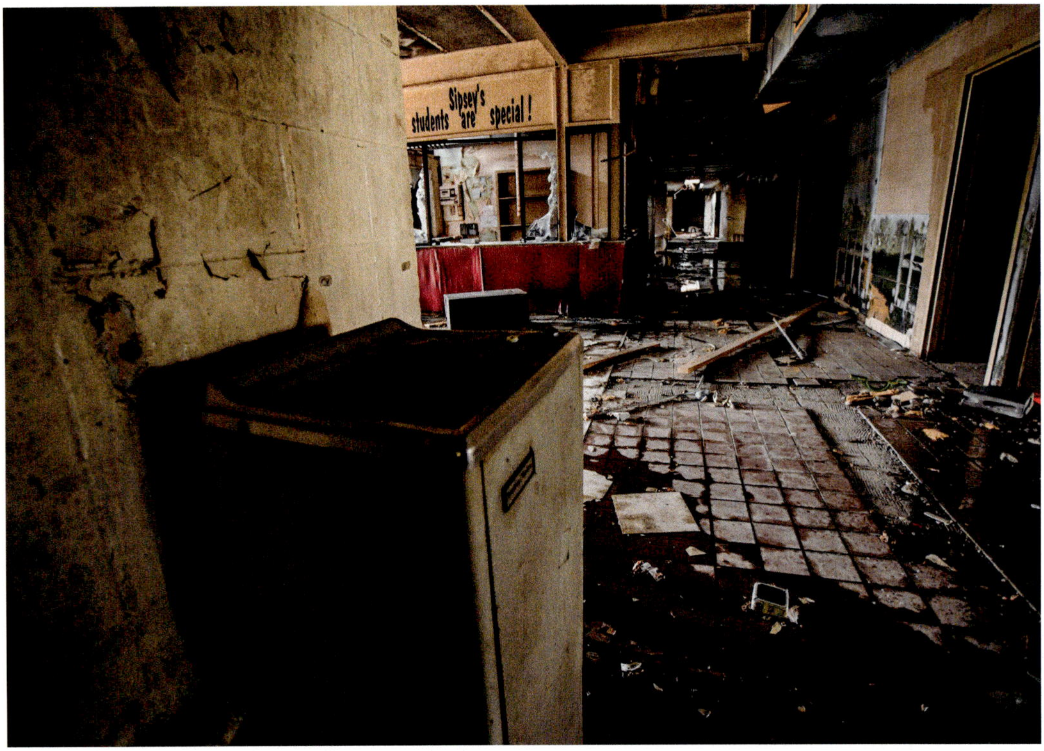

A water fountain at the school entrance.

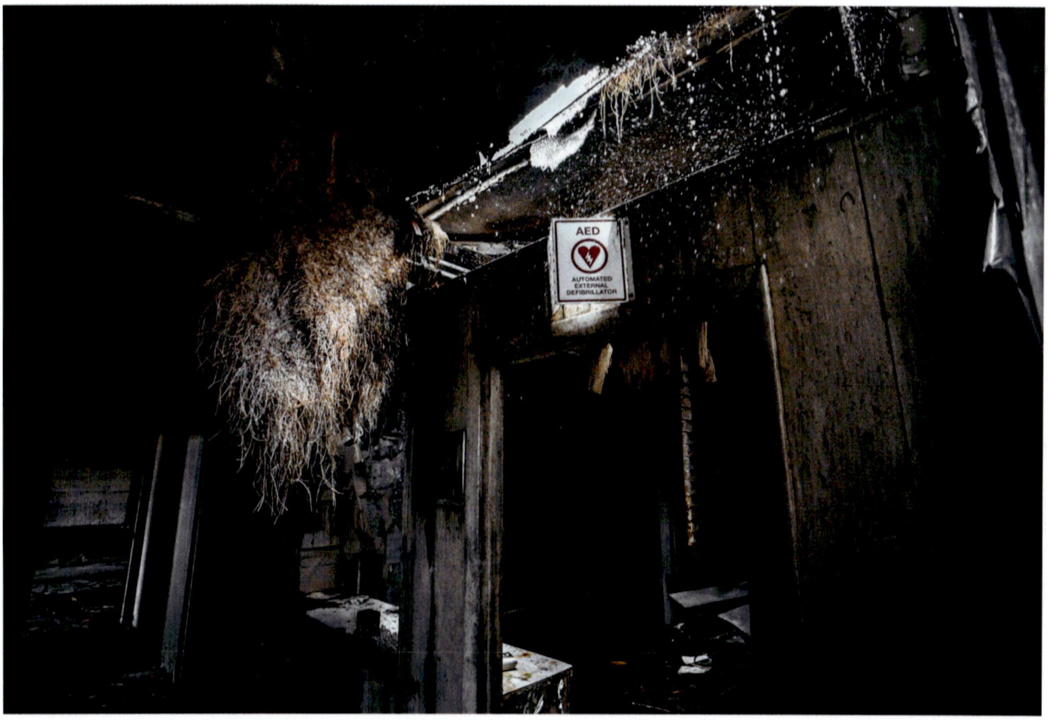

Water and insulation leaks through the ceiling inside the main office.

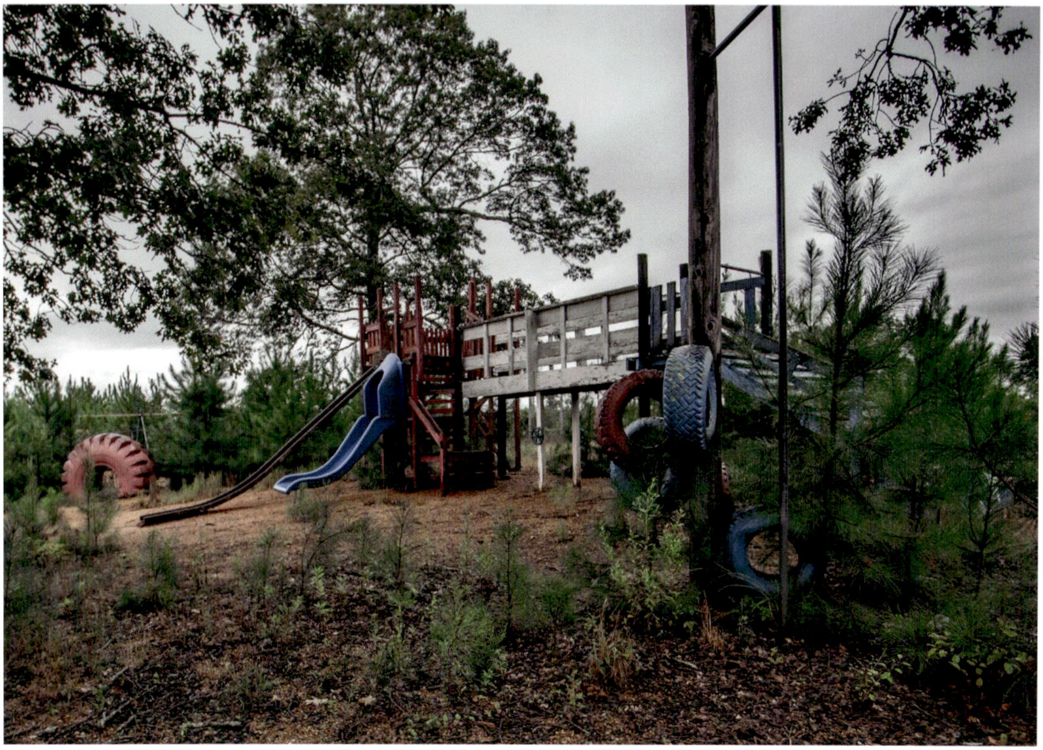

The playground still stands although almost completely surrounded by pine trees.

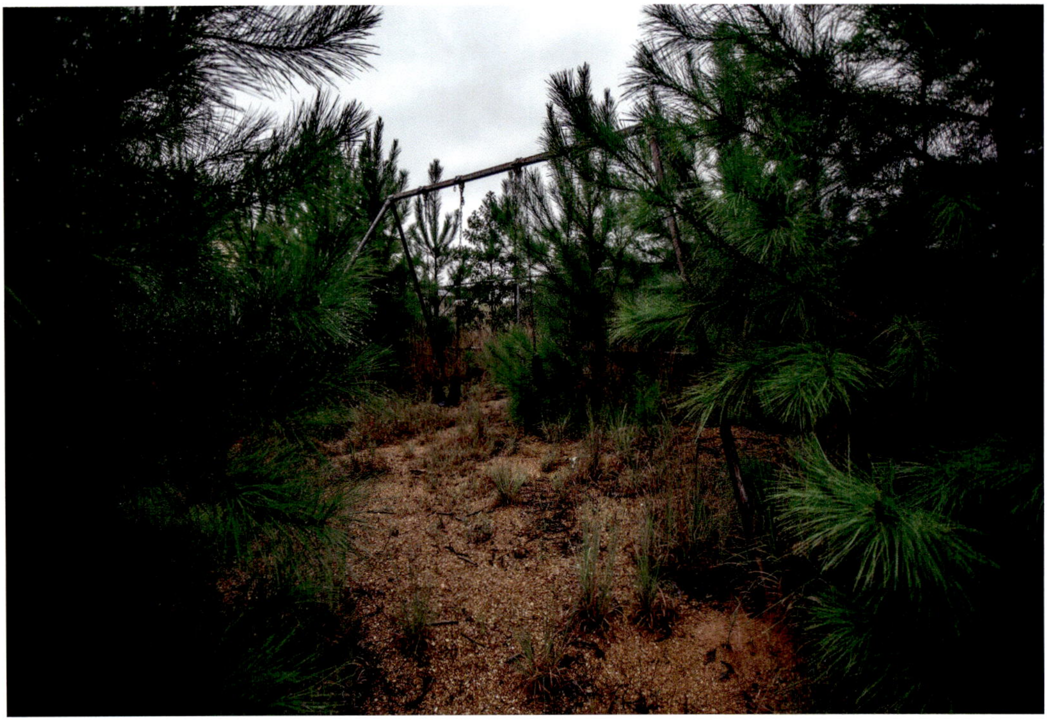

A swing set hiding in the trees.

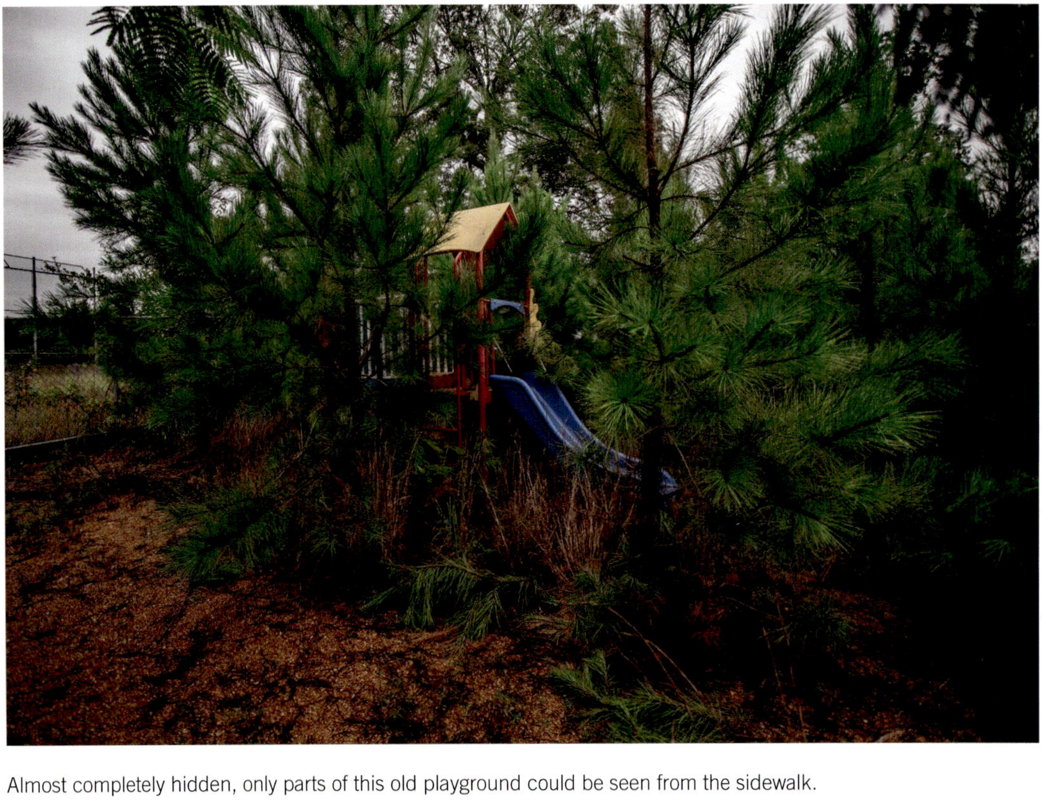

Almost completely hidden, only parts of this old playground could be seen from the sidewalk.

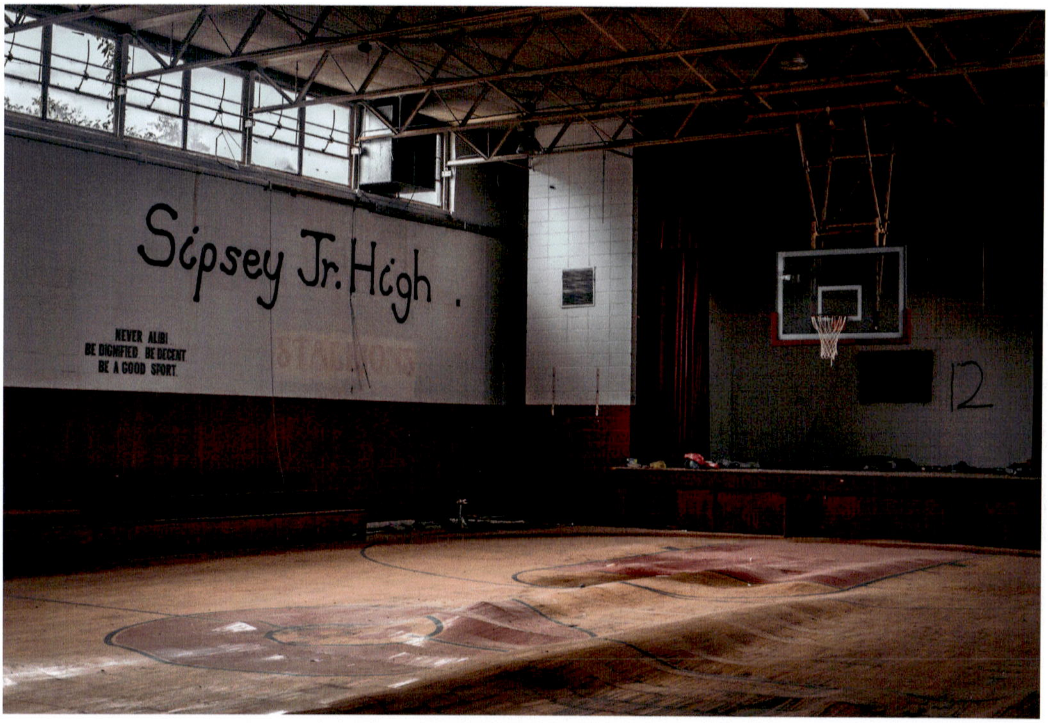

The hardwood floor of the gym rising up off the foundation in rows.

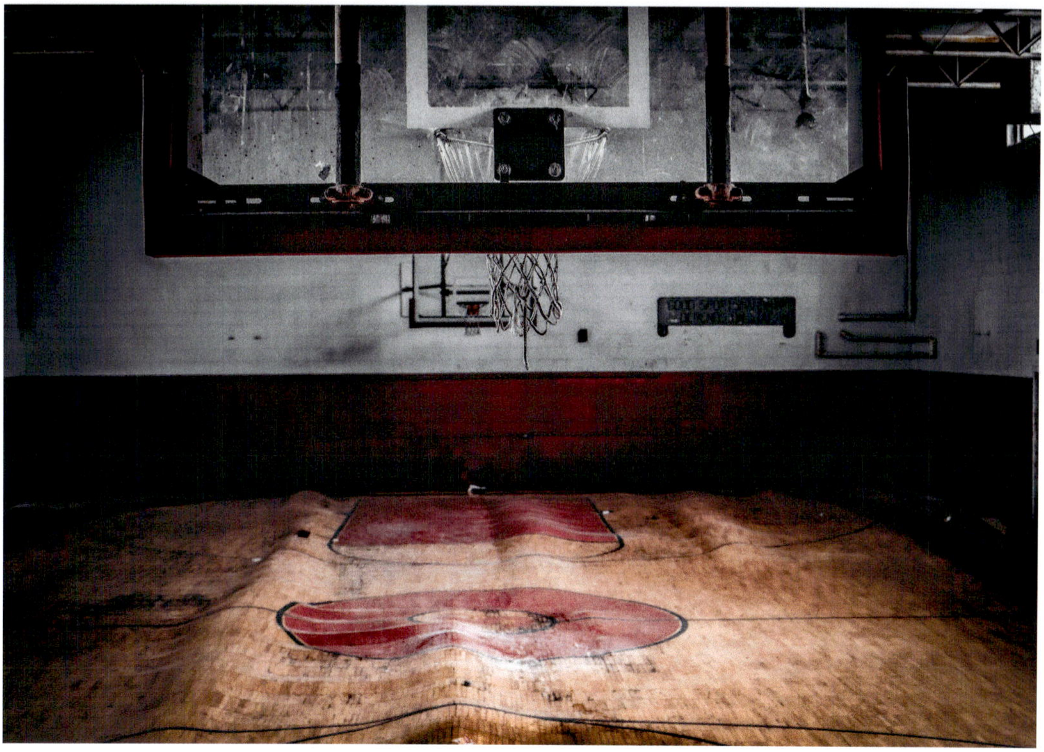

A different angle of the gym shows just how warped the floor has become.

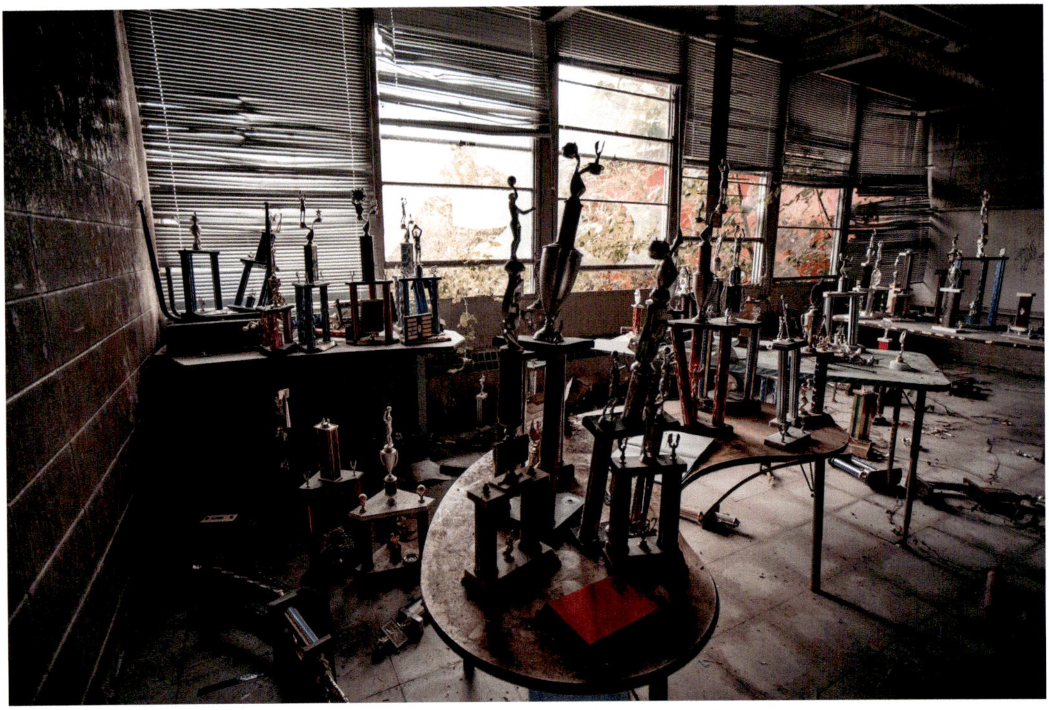

Trophies stored away in the back of a classroom.

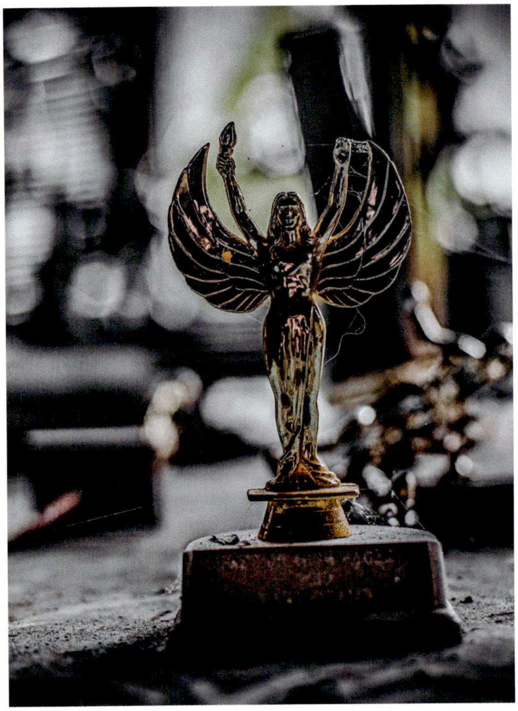

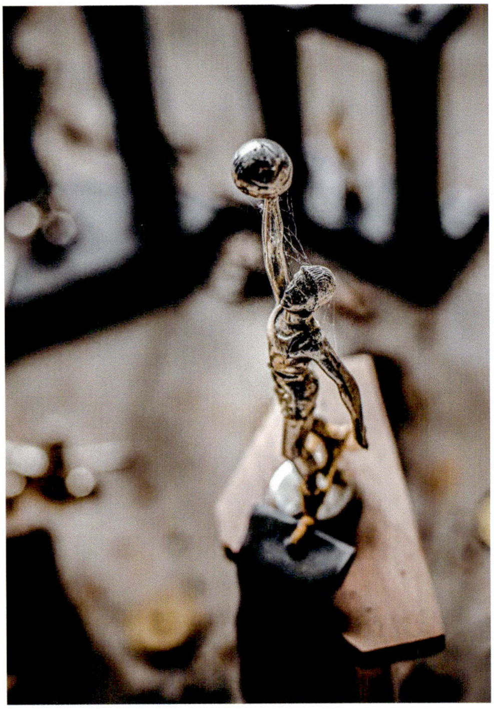

Above left: Dust and cobwebs cover the trophies.

Above right: A basketball trophy with cobwebs left behind.

6

INDUSTRIAL EXPLORATION

Y'all are gonna get hurt doing this one day!" I hear so often from family and friends. I do not give locations out for many reasons. In most cases, it is because one person will tell a friend who will in turn tell a friend and eventually someone who will damage or plunder these places will come along. In some cases, it is out of respect for the family. In this case, it is because after years of neglect, these already dangerous places have become even more of a liability. Industrial facilities are some of the most frightening to explore. A nail slipping from a board or a step rotted through just enough and an explorer can find themselves in a potentially deadly situation. One of the most beautiful factories I have visited has a second story with amazing hardwood flooring. The almost completely rotted floor still has the lines painted on it where the factory workers were supposed to stand. The problem with the place is that only a fraction of the support for that floor still remains.

Many of these industrial complexes are on the edges of large towns due to them being an eyesore. This also leads to wildlife taking back over. Birds nest atop the high steel skeletons of once thriving operations. Deer graze in the edge of the fields and occasionally dart across the mostly deteriorated road systems.

Rust covers the metal on the inside. Stagnant pools of water fill tunnel systems. Graffiti covers the walls. Areas are heavily vandalized. Signs this now vacant building once employed incredible amounts of people are often found only in restrooms and break rooms because the work areas are rarely left with any hint of human interactions. This lack of signs of human involvement and the dangers are the main reasons I do not explore industrial complexes often.

I have found that most of these closures are due to competitors being able to supply the product either more reliably or at a faster pace. When these places close, you hear about it on the news because of the number of employees that have to find other means of employment. These are huge employers. Sometimes one closing can severely handicap a community's economy. There are a few cases I have seen where an entire town has seen a mass exodus due to industrial complexes being shut down or closing. When this happens, there are usually a lot of expensive properties being sold remarkably cheap and bought by lower income families. The payments and costs of the upkeep become too much of a burden and that leads to even more foreclosures and abandonment in the town. One particular town in the southern half of Alabama was once one of the wealthiest until the mining industry there folded and now, the city is full of abandoned homes that in most neighborhoods across the state would be considered extremely high end.

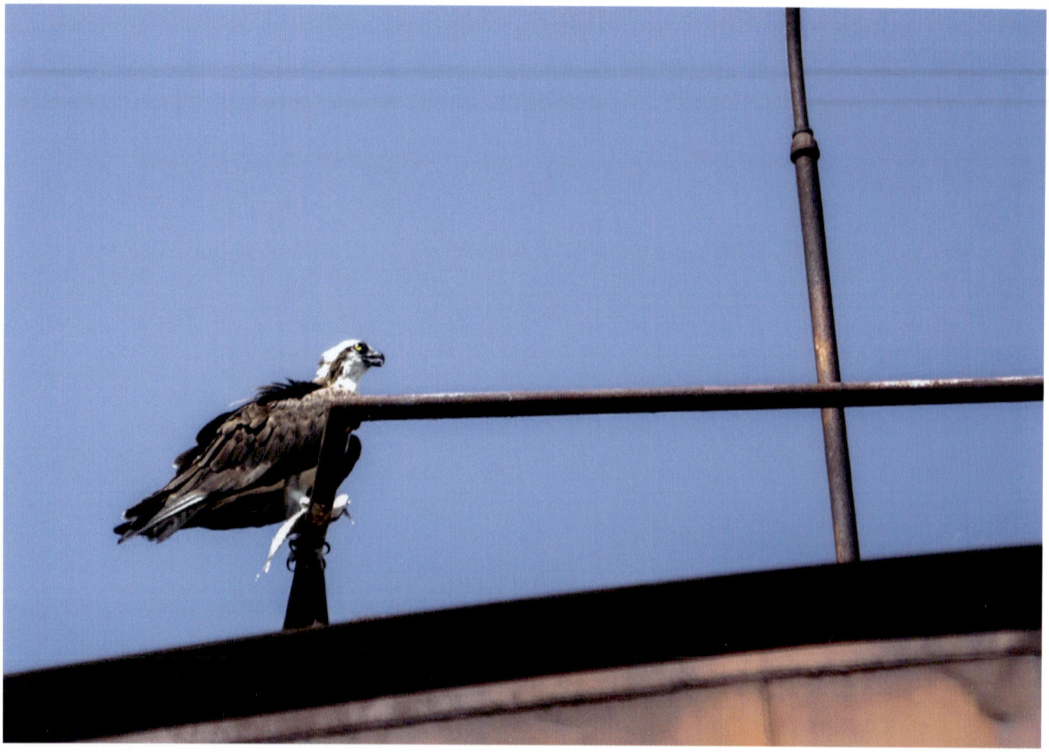

An osprey carrying a fish perches on top of the old silo.

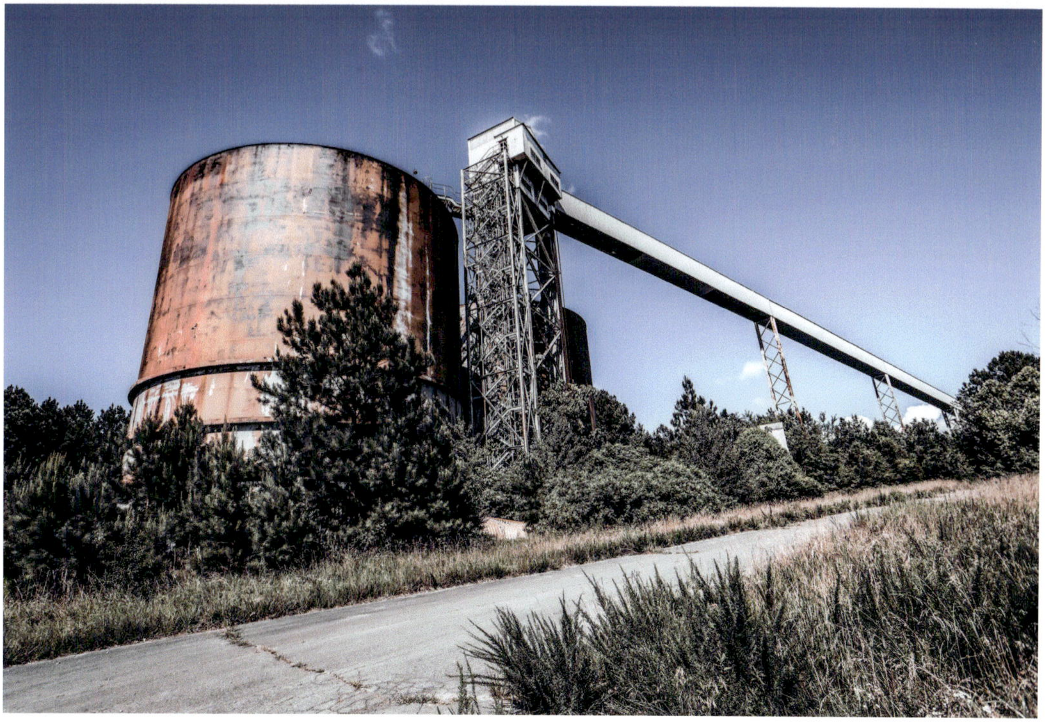

This industrial park still has many functional businesses but some wait for demolition.

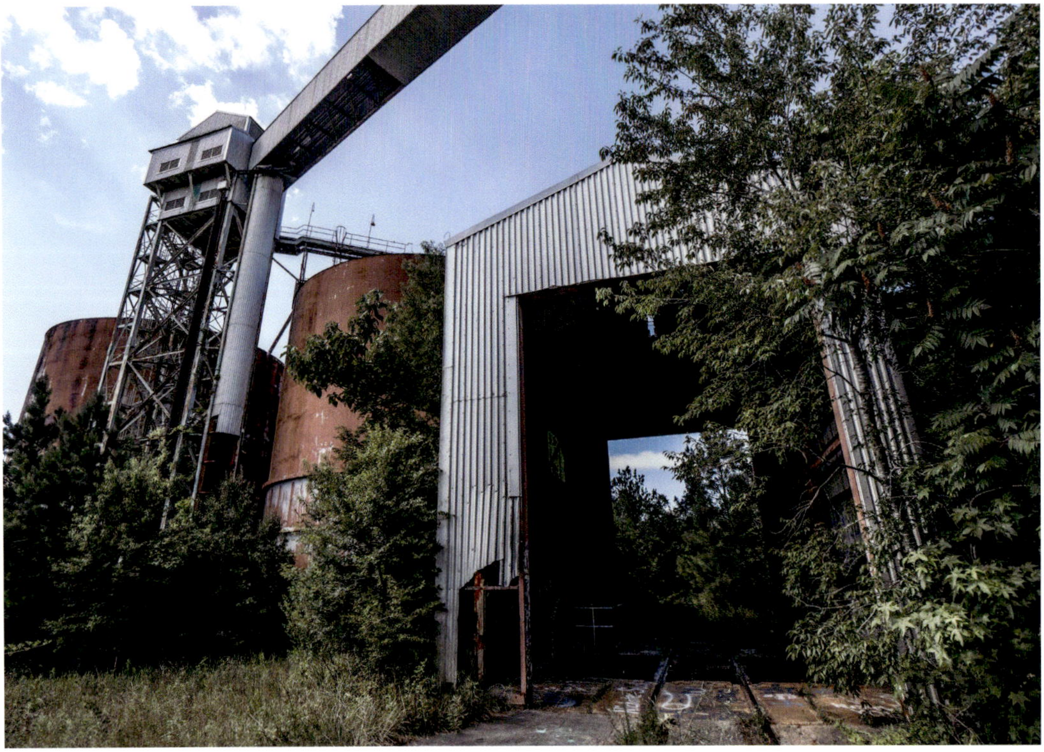

The building where train carts were loaded is now covered in brush and graffiti.

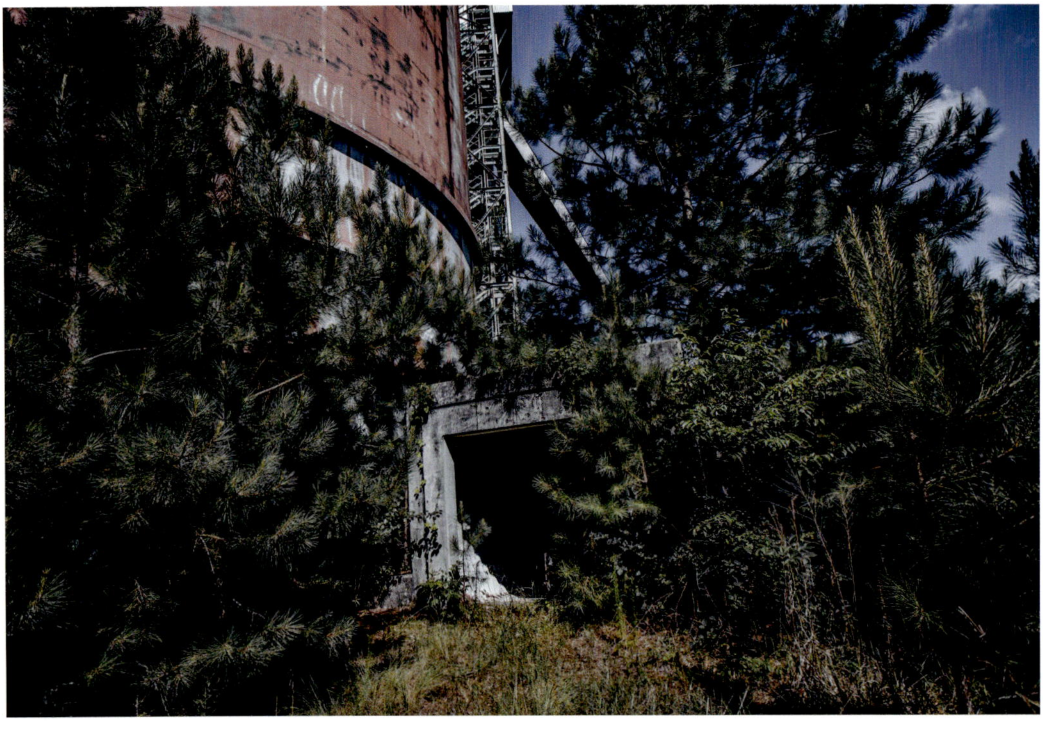

An opening to an underground tunnel with a large conveyor belt.

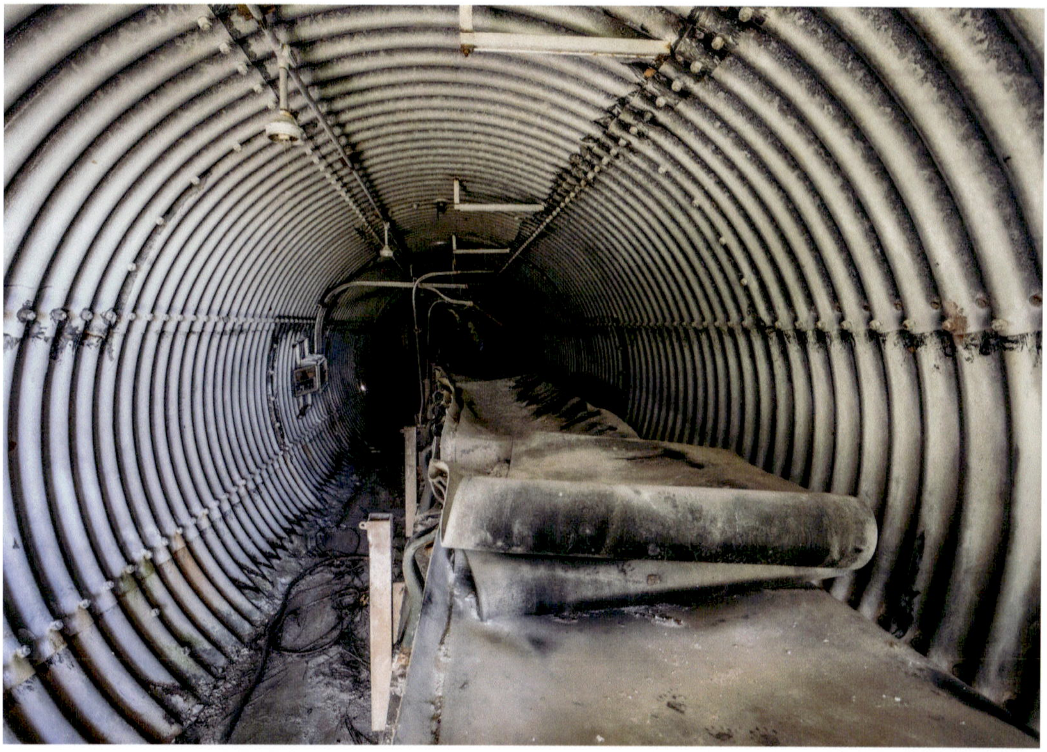

The conveyor belt inside the tunnel leads to an underground pool of water.

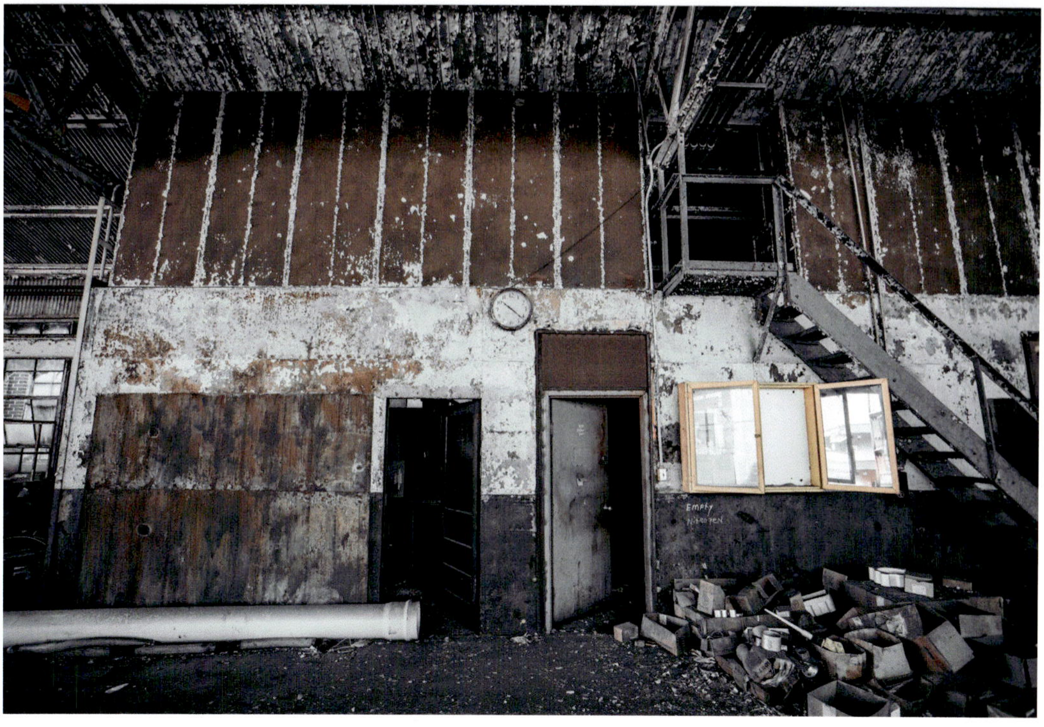

A clock and bulletin board inside an old factory.

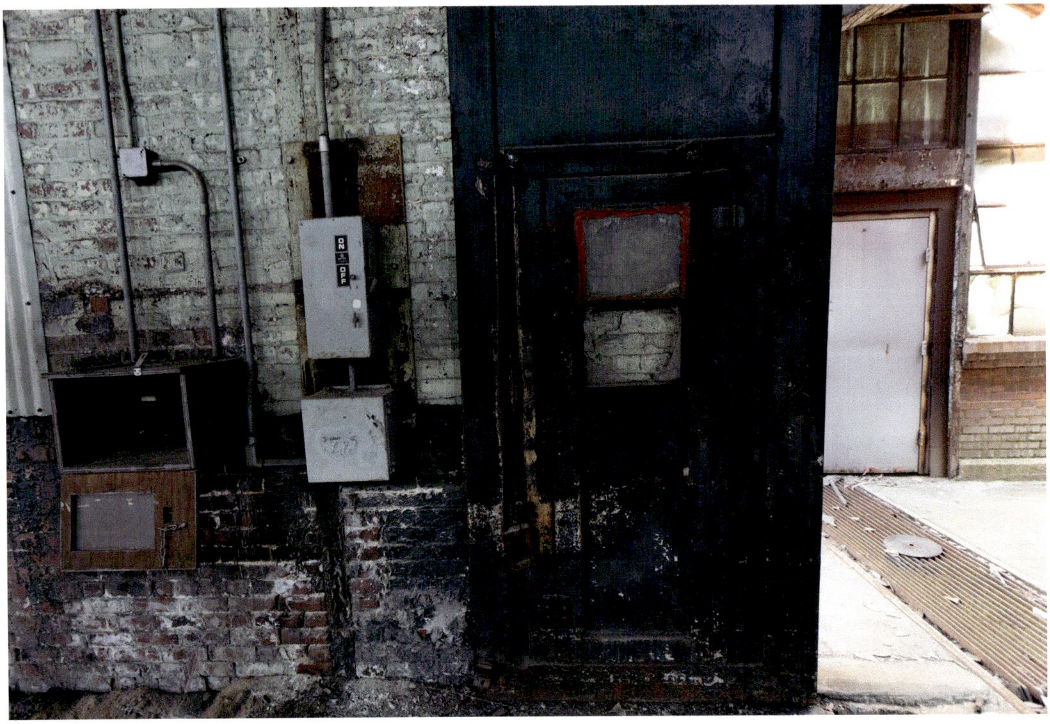

An old breaker box inside the factory.

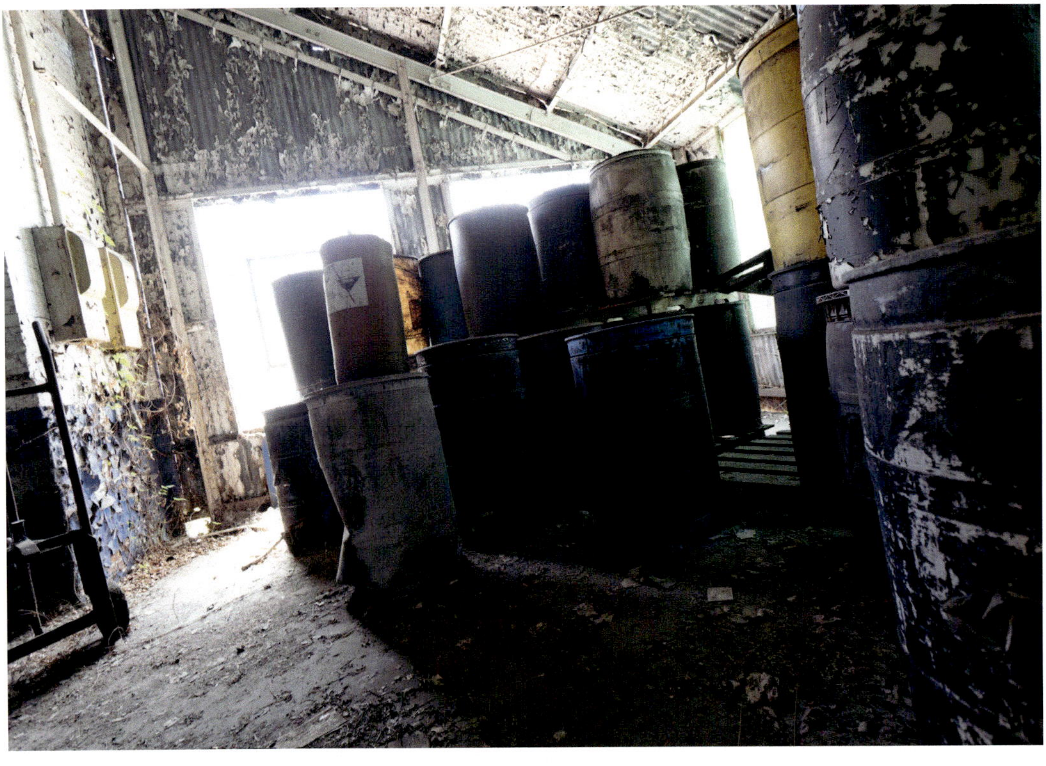

Drums of oil and other chemicals are still left behind.

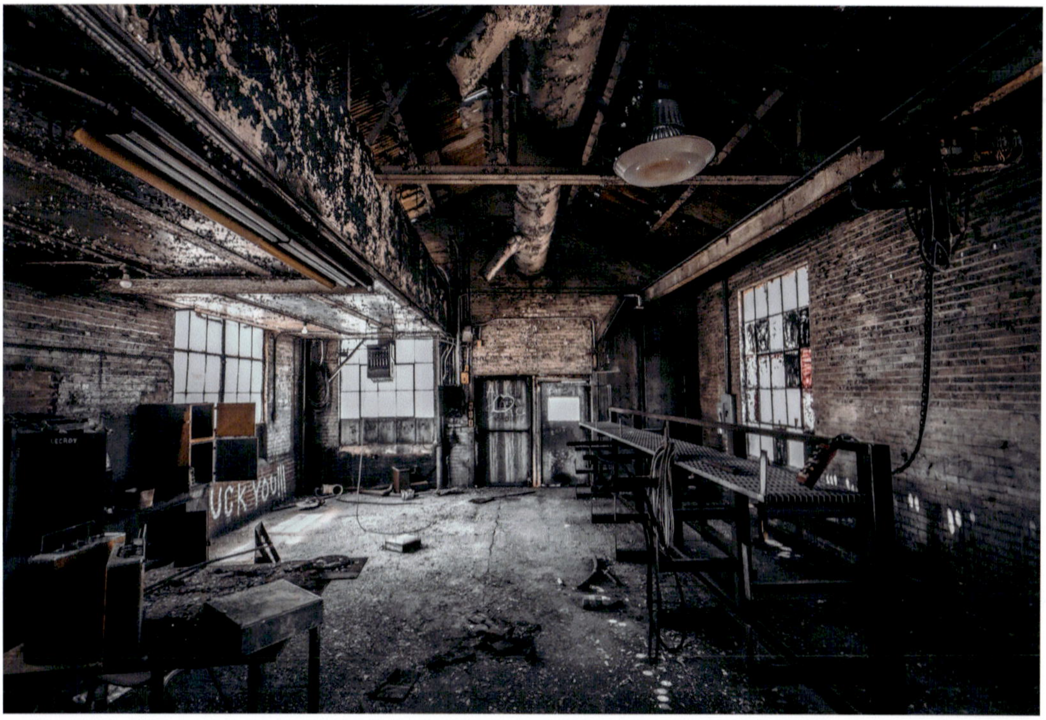

Everywhere you turn in this old factory feels like a potential injury.

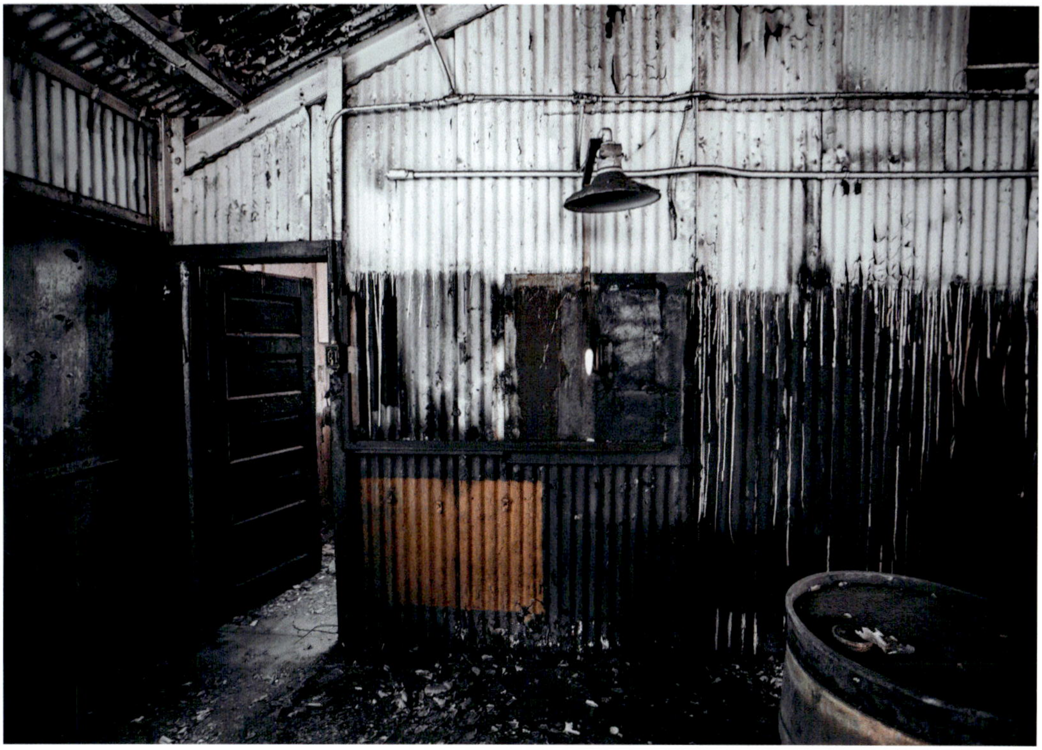

An emergency wash station located near the drums of chemicals.

7

A DIFFERENT TIME

Sometimes people let once treasured homes go when they are forced to let people who lived there go. Slightly off an old county backroad that goes hours without any traffic sits an old country house built in the 1960s with a yard that is still maintained by neighbors. If not for the boards on the windows and the collapsing roof, this house may pass as a place someone still calls home.

The outside bears all the marks of a 1960s or early '70s country home including the almost mandatory blue ceiling on the front porch. To those unfamiliar with this color, its use in southern architecture has dark and troubling roots. It was originally used by slaves in the southeast to ward off spirits or ghosts. The slaves believed the color would fool ghosts into thinking it was sky and make them pass through it. This is also the reason it is often used to deter wasps and spiders from building nests and webs. The popularity of the color before the Civil War had major implications on slavery due to it being derived from a plant harvested entirely in the southeastern states.

A porch swing creaks as it brushes against an overgrown holly bush. Stepping inside this house immediately feels like you have travelled back in time. The scent that wafts out of the house when you open the front door is unexpected. Usually when going into a house that has been stagnant for even a few months, you can smell the lack of air circulation, mold, and dust, but this house is different. I learn later that it has been thirty years since the owner walked through that front door and what I can only imagine is the smell of her perfume still lives here. The condition of the interior shows the time that has passed since the owner died on the couch, but it is almost impossible to shake the feeling that the house could never really belong to anyone else.

The decomposition stains on the couch left in the living room prove that the family had no intention of ever doing much with the residence. A constant reminder to anyone who stepped foot inside, this place became stuck in time the day she died. The living room mantel adorned with collectibles that no doubt meant something to her and three pictures of celebrities: Bob Hope, Henry Fonda, and Tyrone Power framed and watching over the living room. I think about how much different the times must have been to hold such high regard for entertainment personalities. Displayed in a way that would lead one to believe they were loved ones, these pictures give a massive glimpse into the woman who lived alone in this house for years.

The furniture and items in the house make the house feel much older than it actually is. I believe this is because people who grew up through the Great Depression tended to keep many items long after their usefulness had run its course. The lack of a television in the living room is another sign of the values held by the owner. Instead, a baby grand piano surrounded by couches and seats is the centerpiece of the room. The only television is tucked away in the corner of a bedroom as if it were an appliance or a tool only used when there is severe weather coming or on a special occasion.

This house, under normal circumstances, could survive much longer than it will. Houses need people just as badly as people need houses. Left to their own devices, a small leak can become a flood and a single drip can eventually rot out an entire room. Walls caving in from a single room can destroy the structural integrity of the entire foundation. The decay never stops in one spot, it spreads. If no one is there to nurture it, a house can quickly turn to rubble. This country home, for at least a little while longer, will provide a glimpse into the life of a woman and where her story ended.

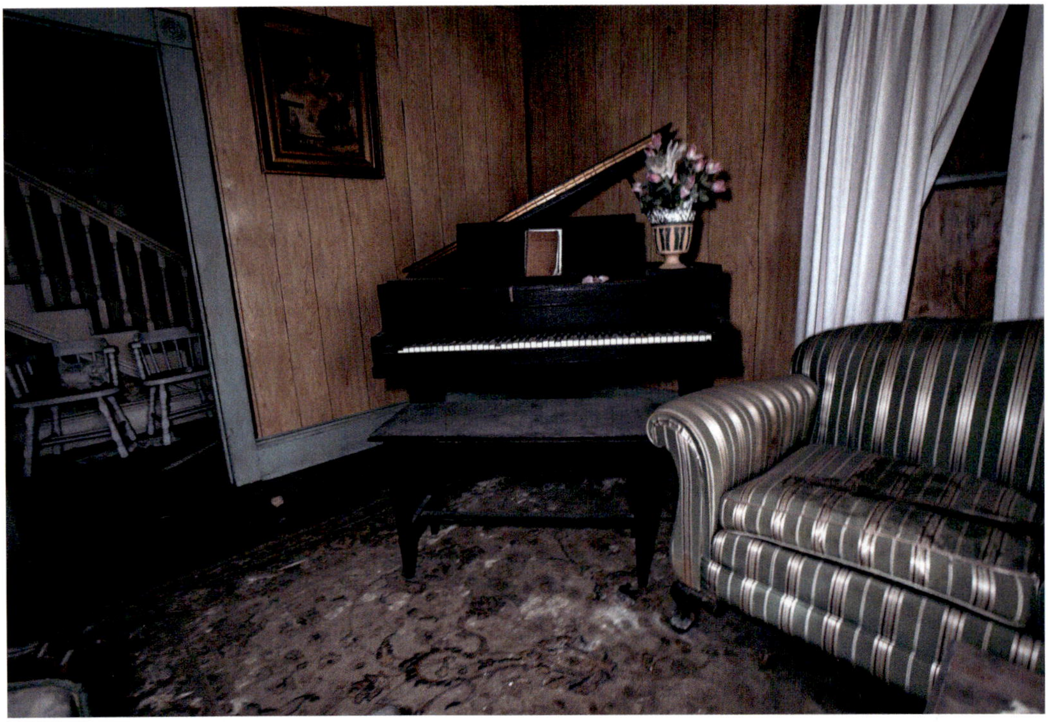

The couch where this woman died still sits in the living room next to the piano.

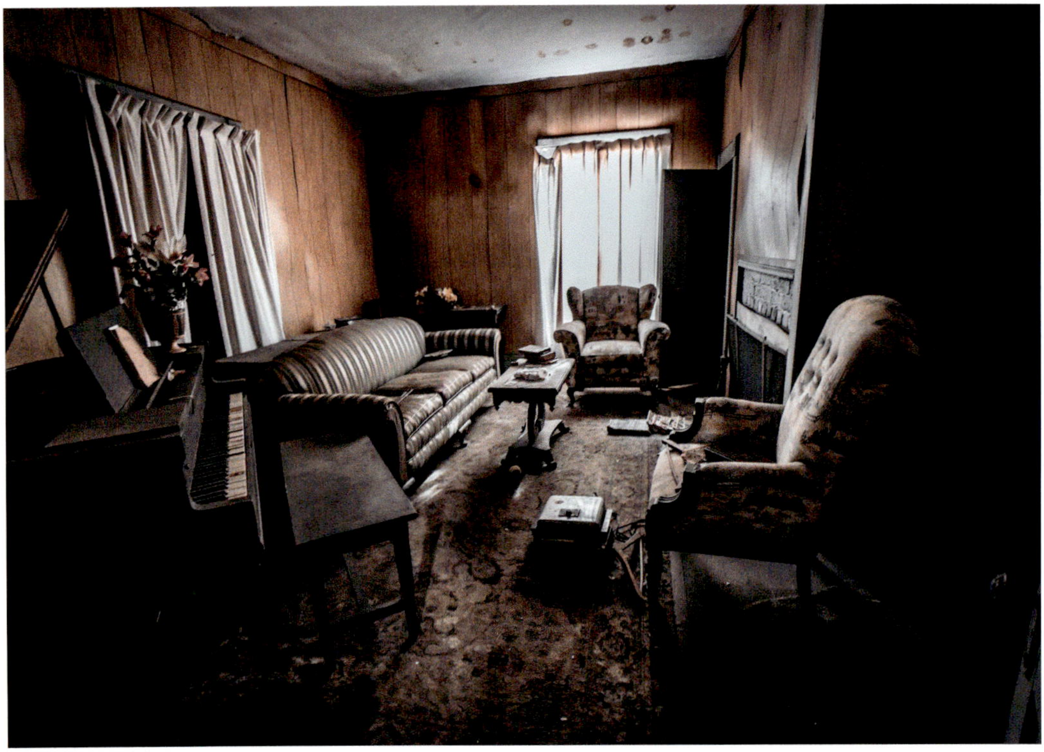

The old furniture still sits the way it did when she died.

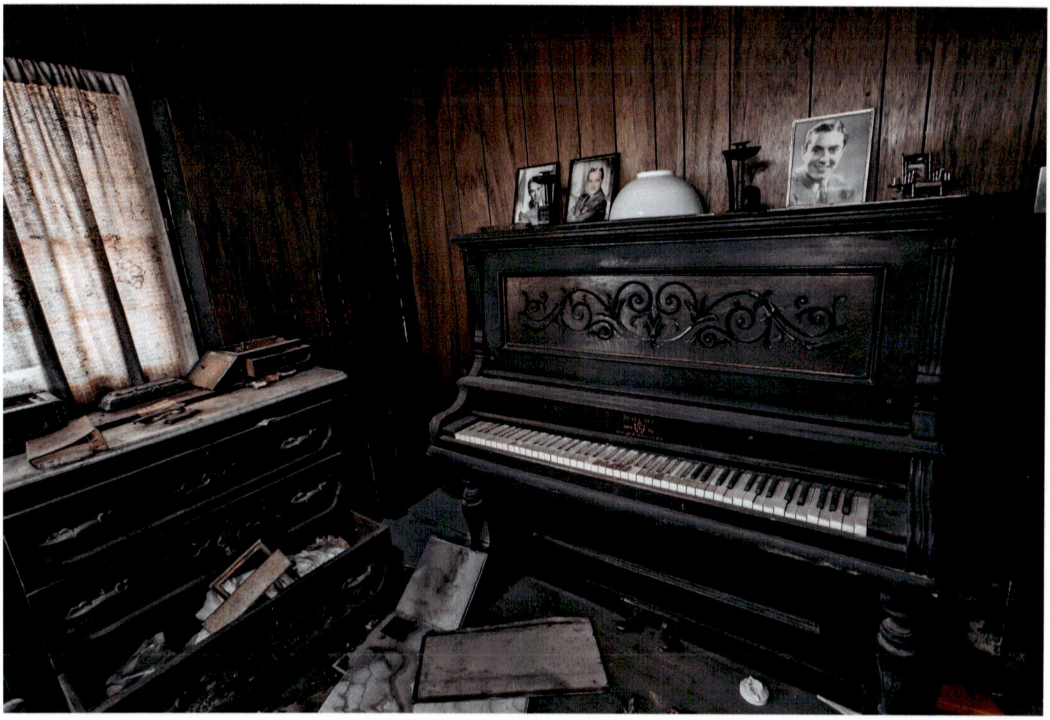

The piano with mementos and pictures of popular celebrities.

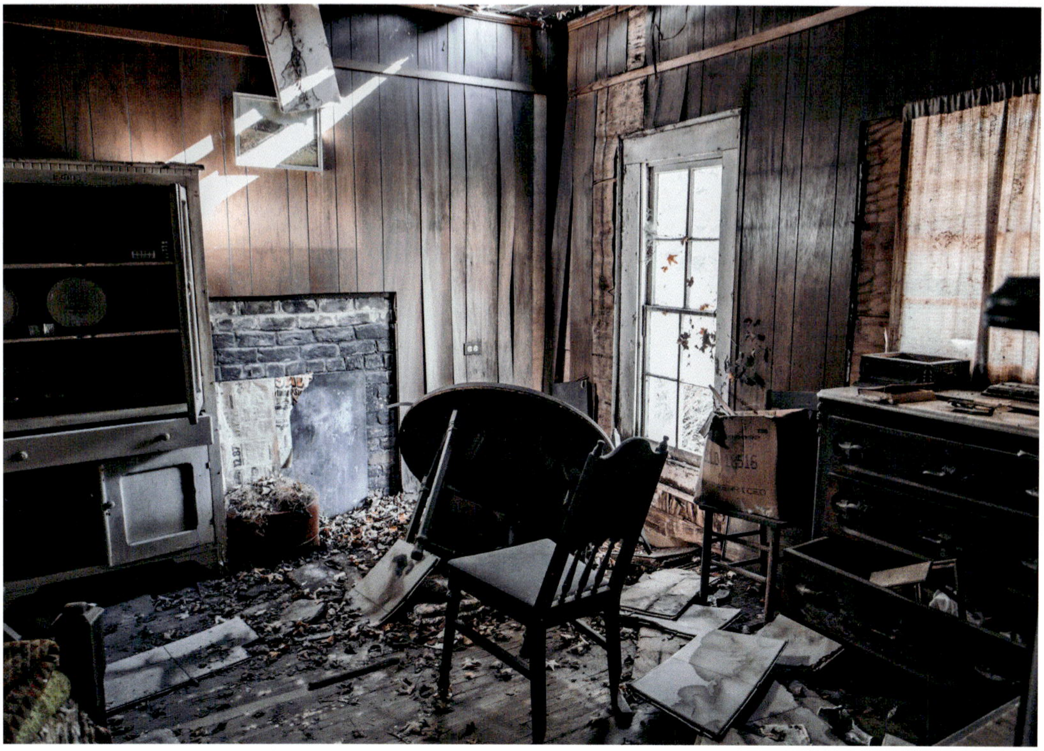

This is the most damaged room in the home. A decayed ceiling lets in elements from the outside.

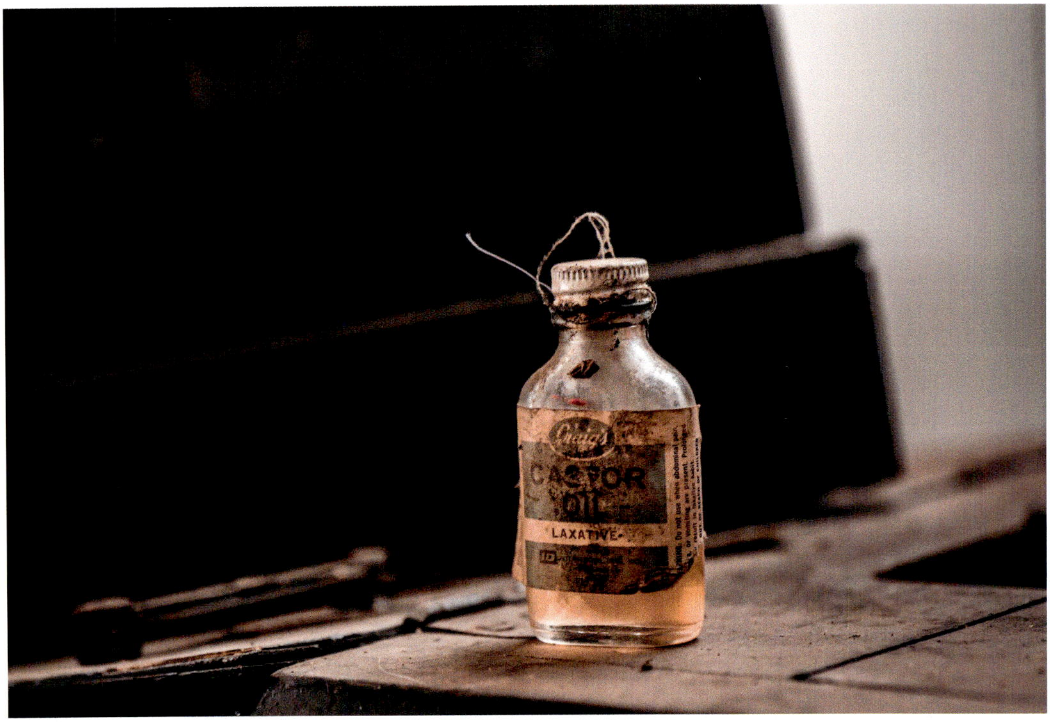

An old bottle of castor oil on the table next to one of the many beds in this home.

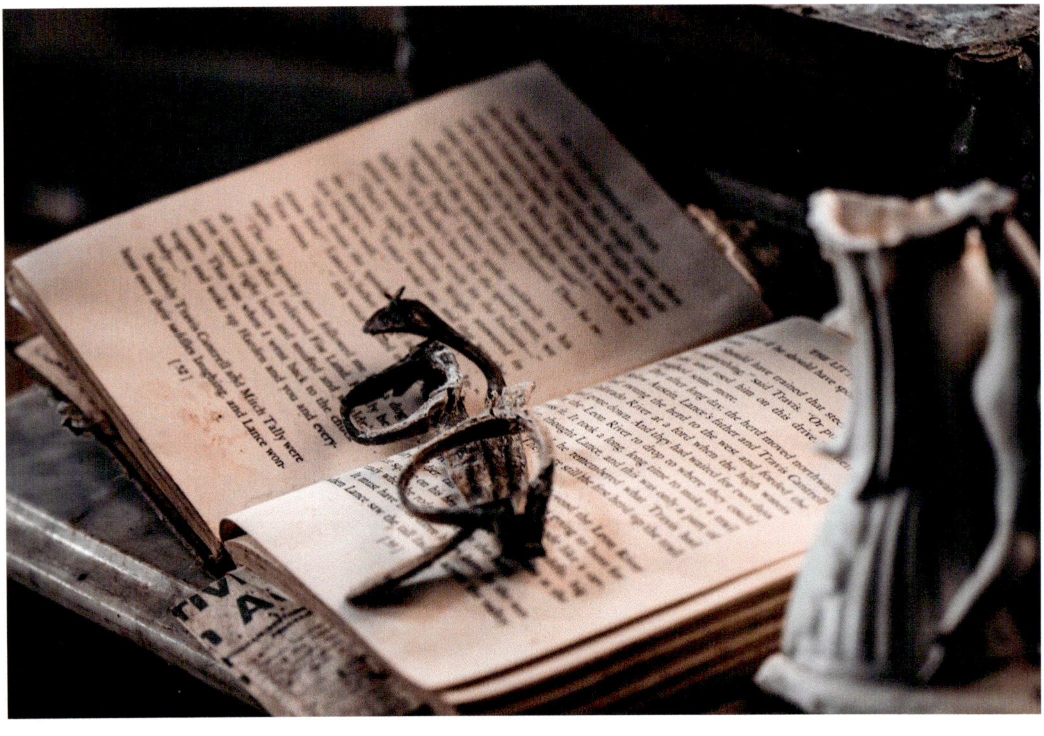

One of many old books found inside the residence, all displayed in a way that makes you believe literature was important to this family.

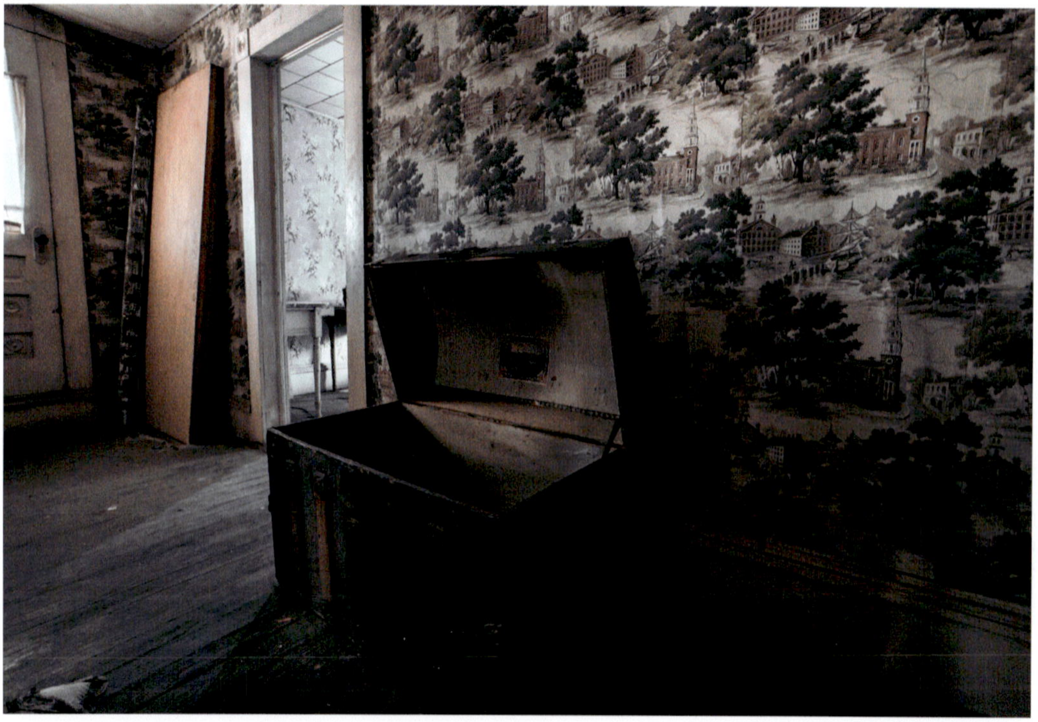

The wallpaper in this house was different in every room.

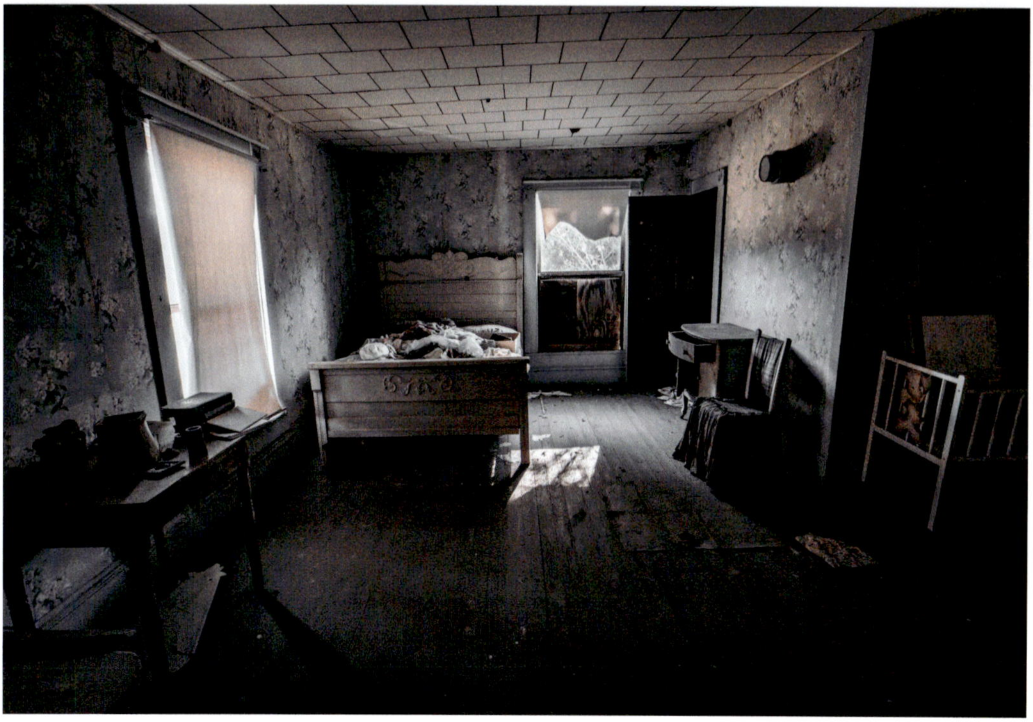

One of the bedrooms still intact with a variety of old furniture including a baby crib.

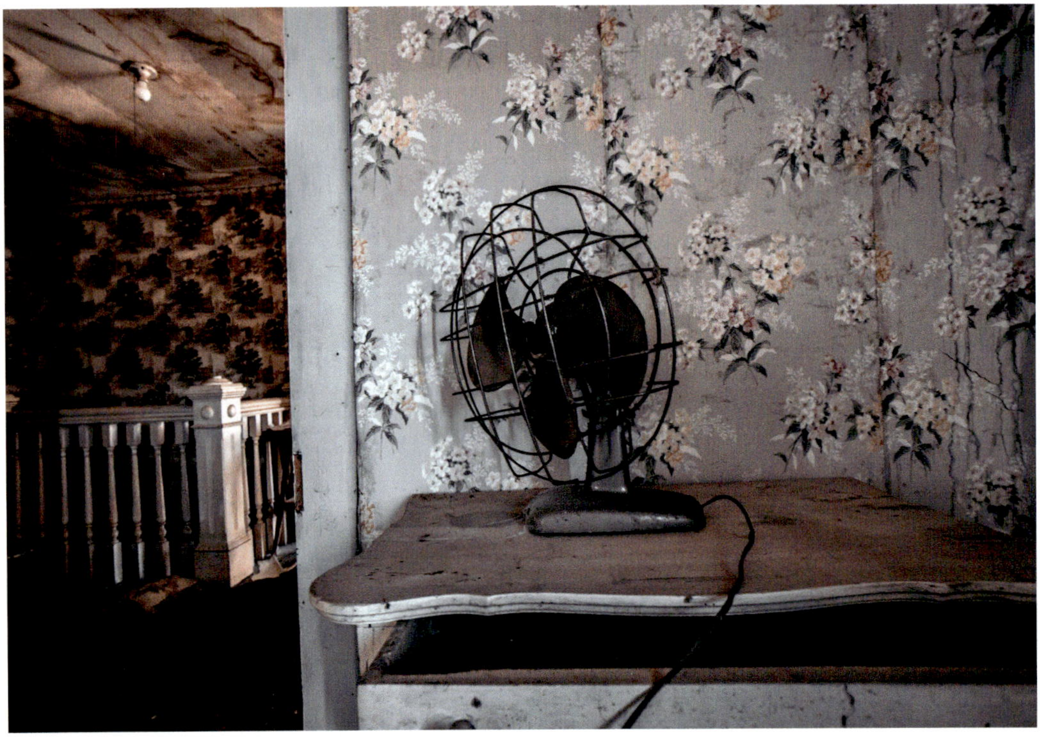

An old fan on a desk in the bedroom.

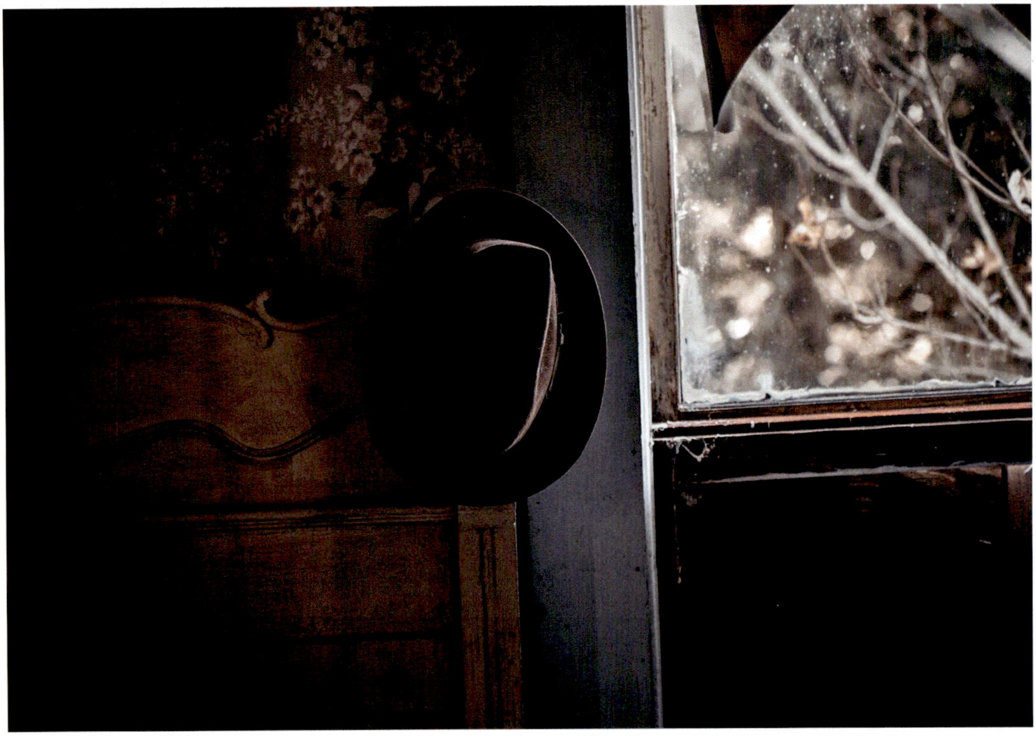

A hat on the bedpost in the upstairs bedroom.

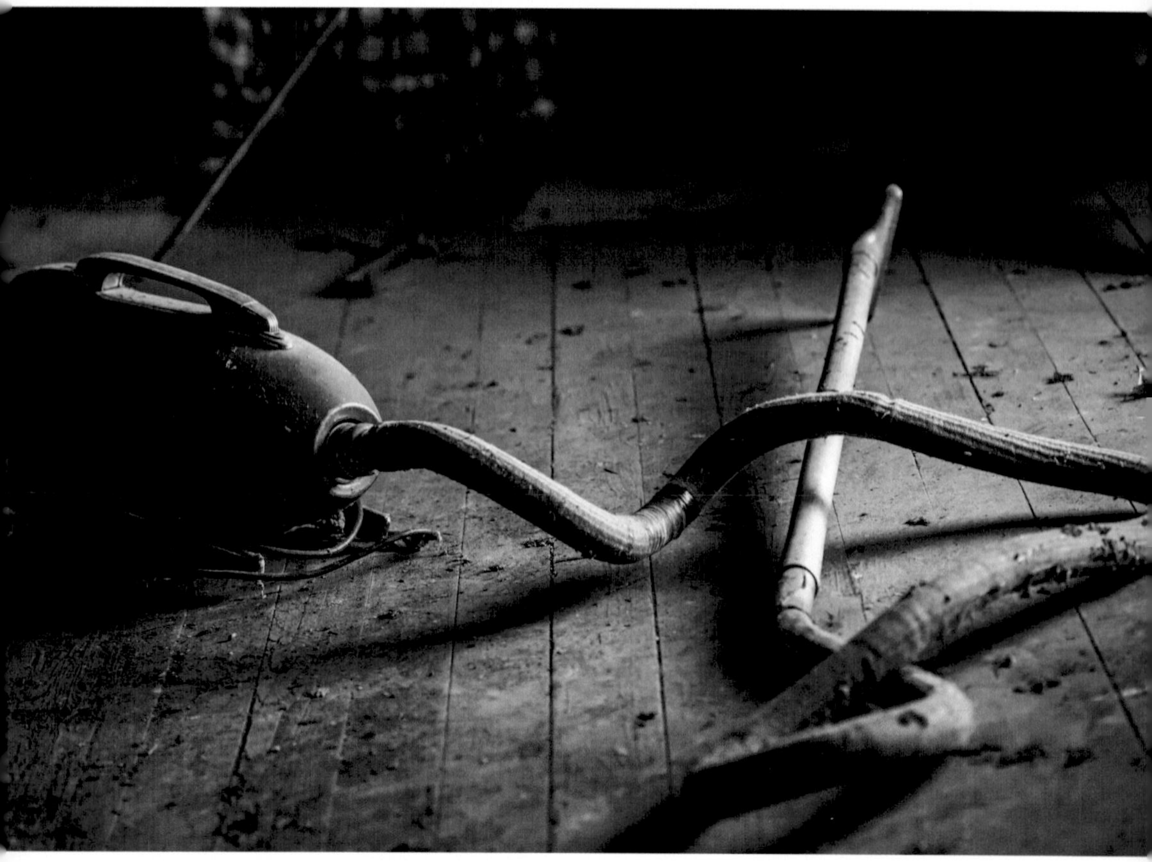

An old vacuum cleaner still left out on the floor.

8

THE ELUSIVE STORIES

Just because you cannot uncover the story does not mean one is not there. I could not give an entire chapter to every house we visited so included a brief version of what is known and some pictures of houses with stories that eluded me. I am sure the stories are out there living through a relative or loved one, but in some scenarios, there were not enough clues to fill in the blanks. I have visited some of the houses multiple times to try and learn what happened, and each time came up empty-handed. One particular house in this set was visited multiple times but the more I explored, the less I knew for certain. I then proceeded with my usual online research and the story became even foggier as the names on the items in the house did not match any of the tax records or information that was available online. My best guess is that it was used as a rental house, but the tenant lived there for a long period of time.

Some of these houses were demolished or destroyed by the elements since my visits. One of my favorite abandoned places, a ceramic shop next to a house, I visited several times and focused on a small portion each time. When I went to take my last set of pictures, it had collapsed. This was a horrible feeling. I never found out enough about the story so all I can do to pass this down the line and hope that my pictures do it justice. I am sure the owner's work lives on in many houses in the small town as I have already found locals who claim to have purchased ceramics from her. I'm sure that her family could tell stories for days but all I could find were these statues she undoubtedly put tons of time and love into.

I can only speculate what makes a person up and walk away, or what drags a family away. I have walked into a house and found dishes on the table like a family sat down and decided in the middle of dinner they needed to move without their belongings. I see piles of toys left in kid's rooms and cannot help but remember that sinking feeling when I was a kid and I lost or broke one of my favorite toys. My father once had to console me after getting a stain on my favorite Jose Canseco t-shirt, but the entire lives of these kids is still sitting here after thirty years. I hope the remnants left in those houses aren't where their stories ended but one thing I have learned is that there is rarely an uplifting story behind those toys left forgotten.

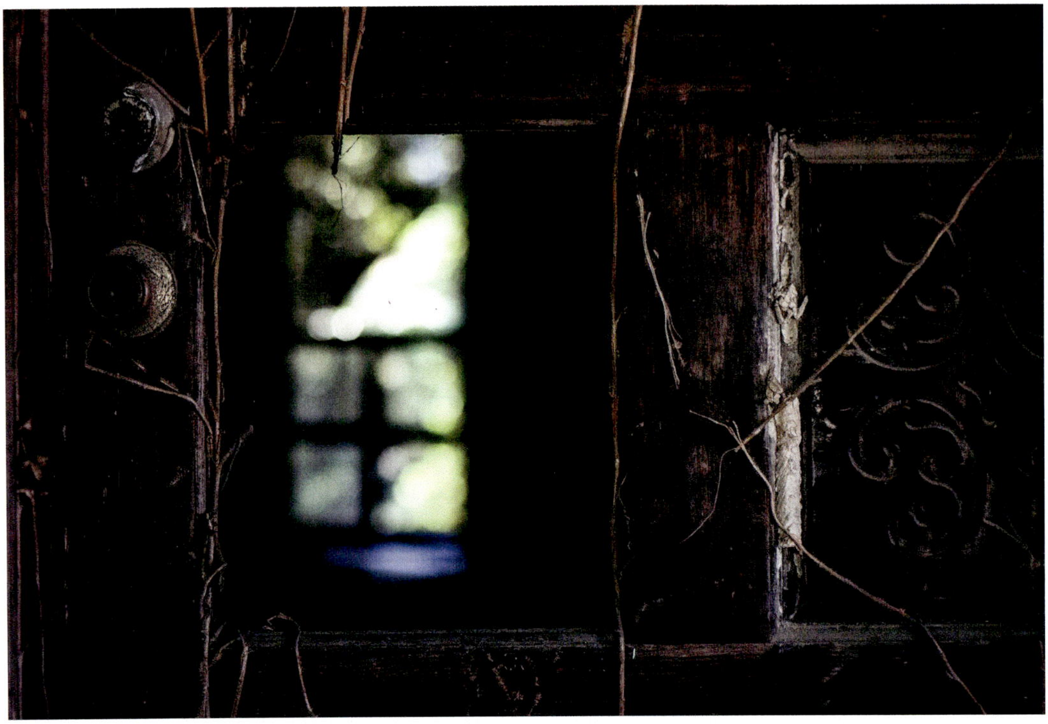

An intricate design on the front door to a home that has been abandoned since the early 1990s.

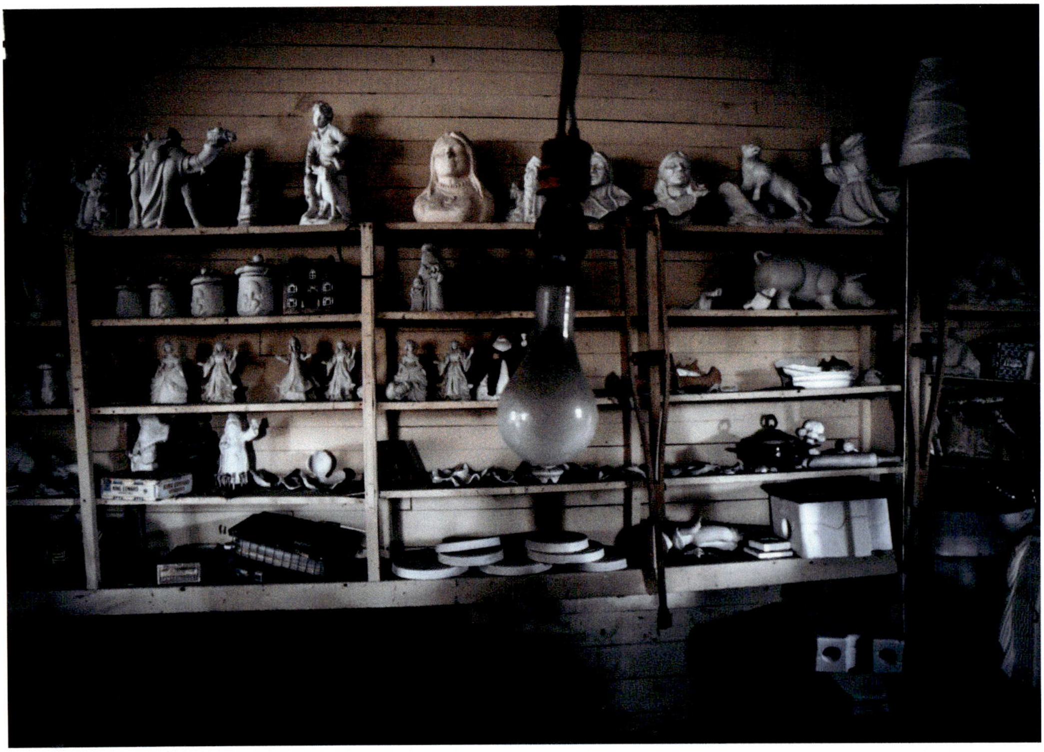

Ceramic figurines lined the wall in the old shop next to the owner's house.

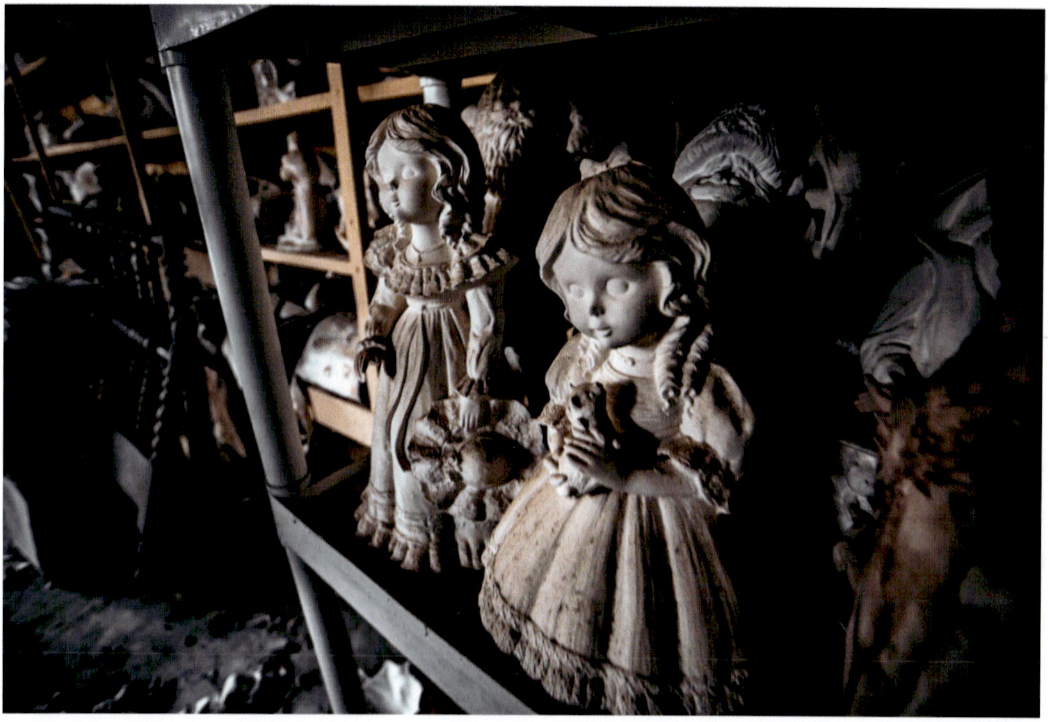

The casts for these figures were all stacked up in the back of the shop.

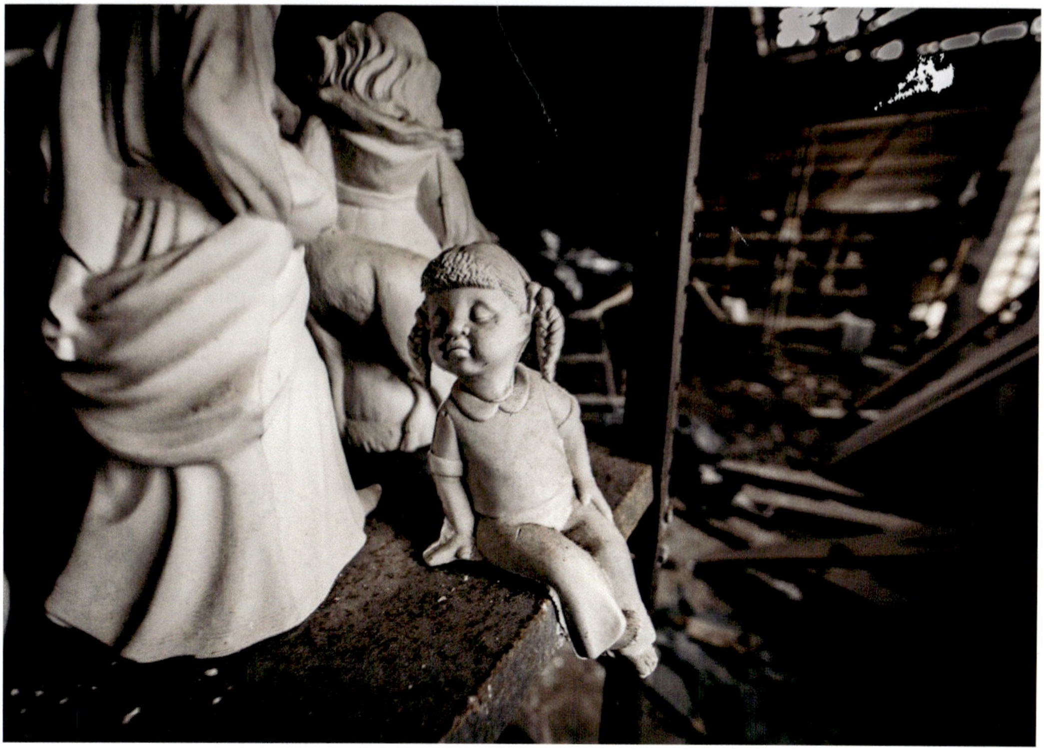

Many were damaged or destroyed before the roof collapsed.

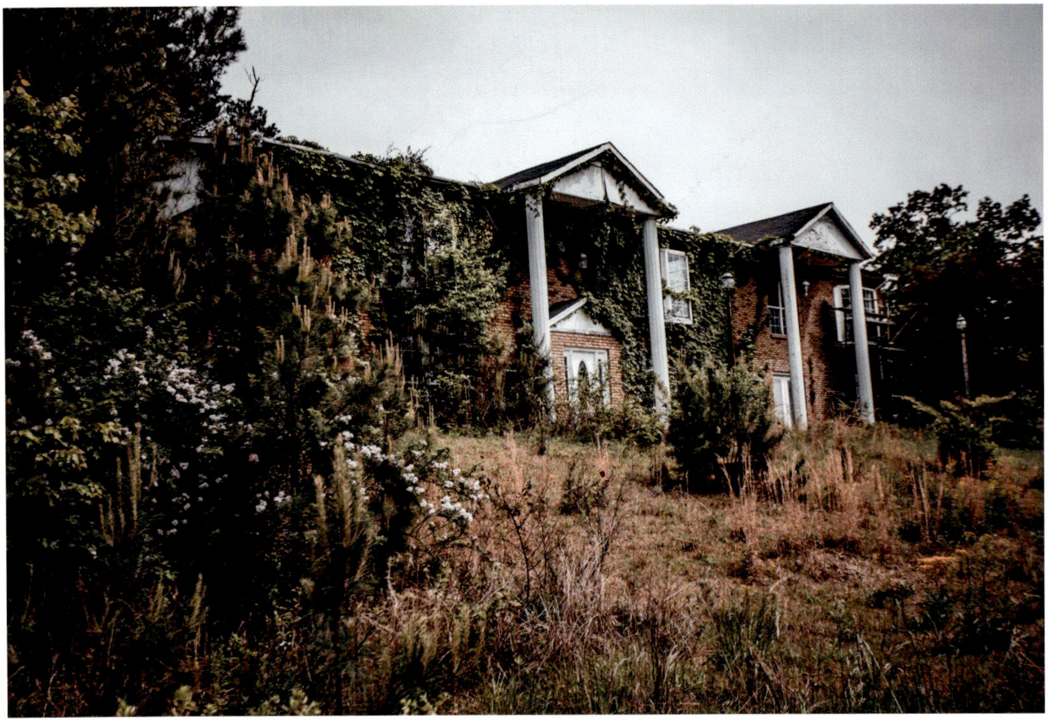

A huge house hidden off the main road appears to have been abandoned while remodeling was being done.

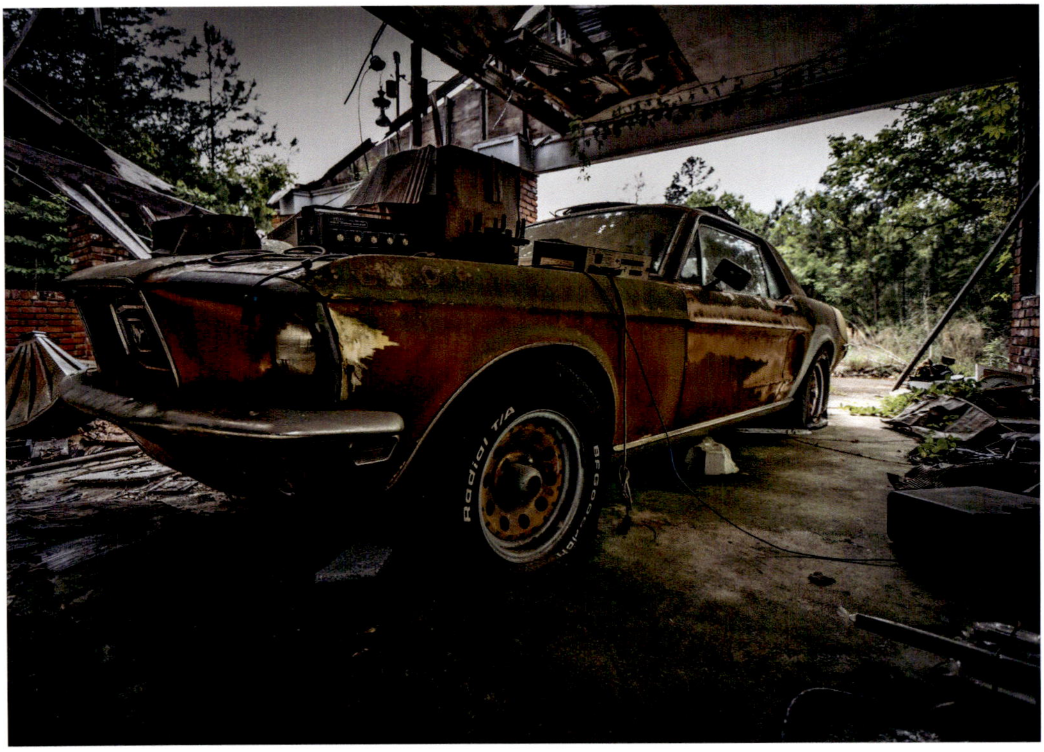

A gold Mustang sits underneath a collapsing carport, soon will be covered by debris.

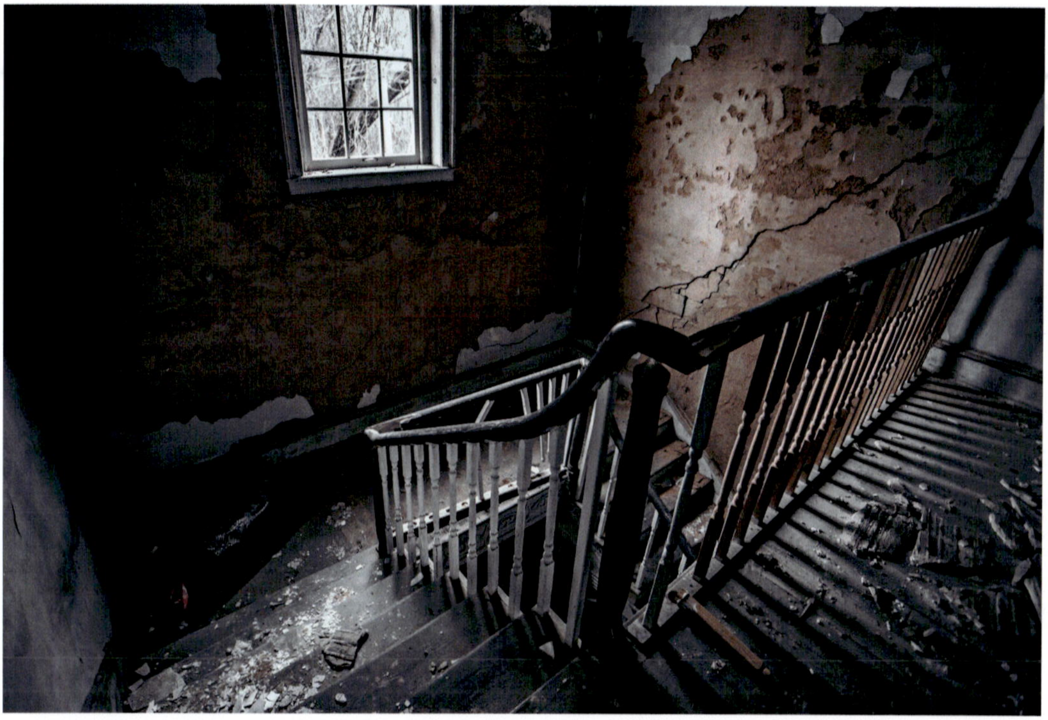

A beautiful stairwell in a large southern home showing its age with a huge crack in the wall.

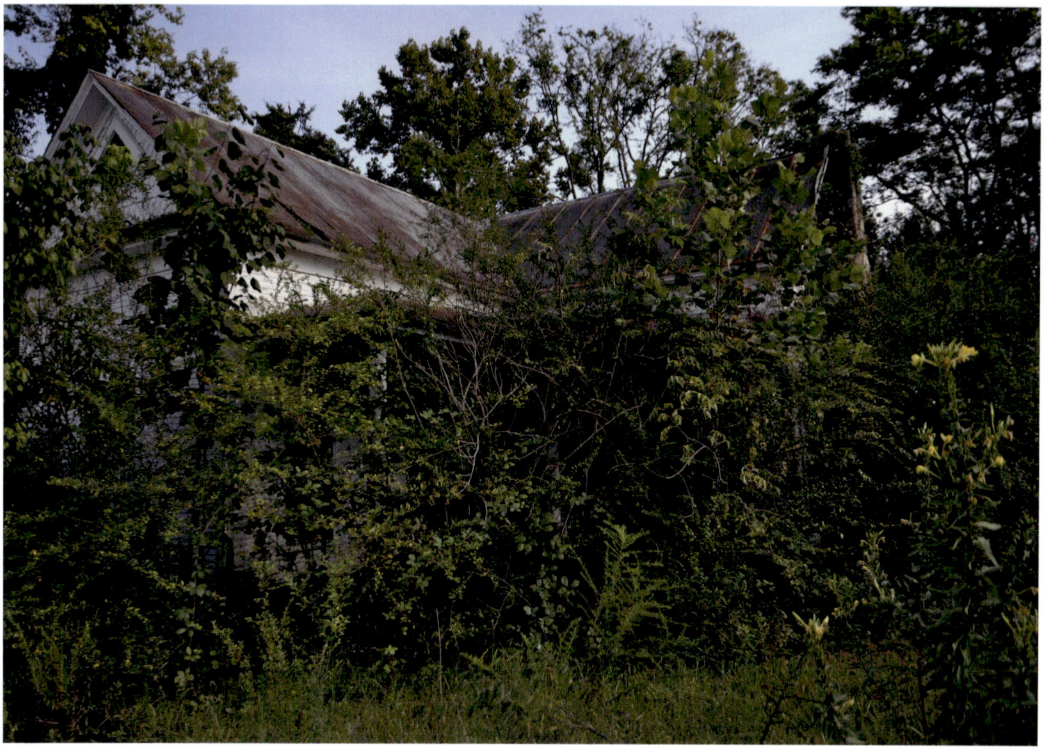

Abandoned in the 1980s, nature has finally started to take this property back.

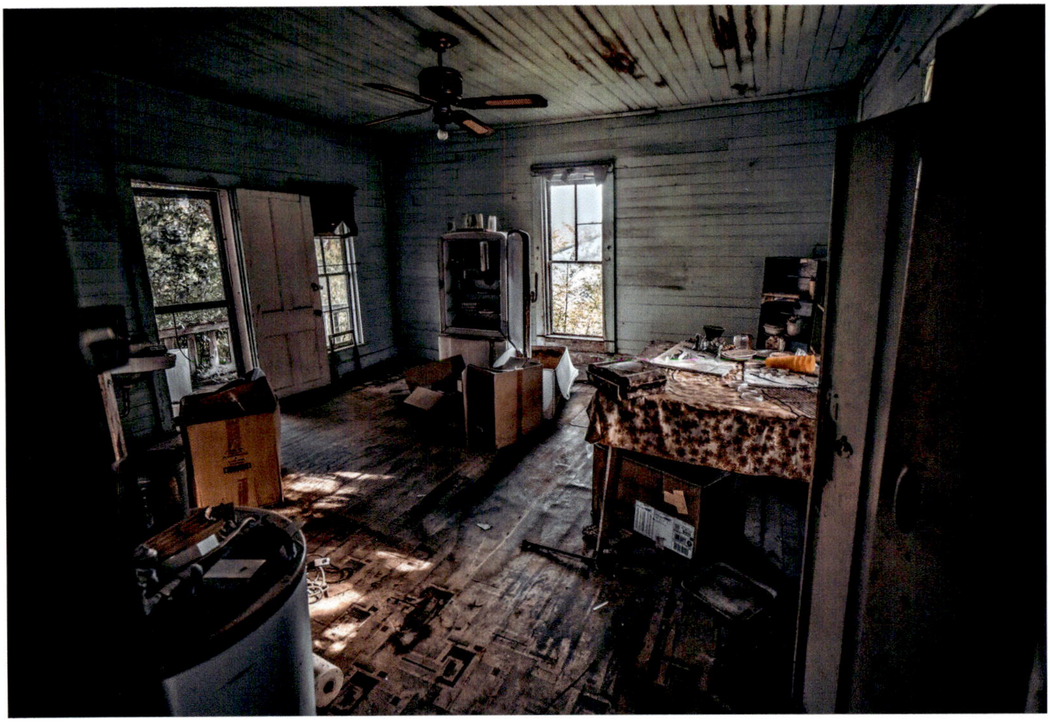

Some old southern homes even used blue paint on the interior.

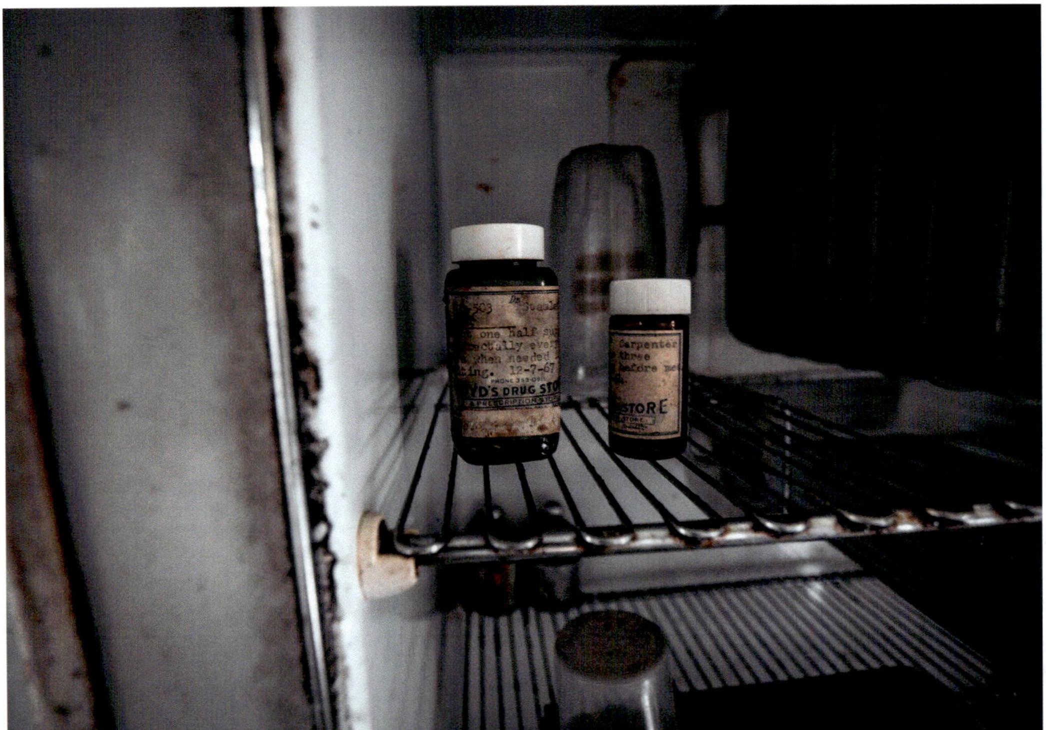

The old fridge still had several prescription medications inside.

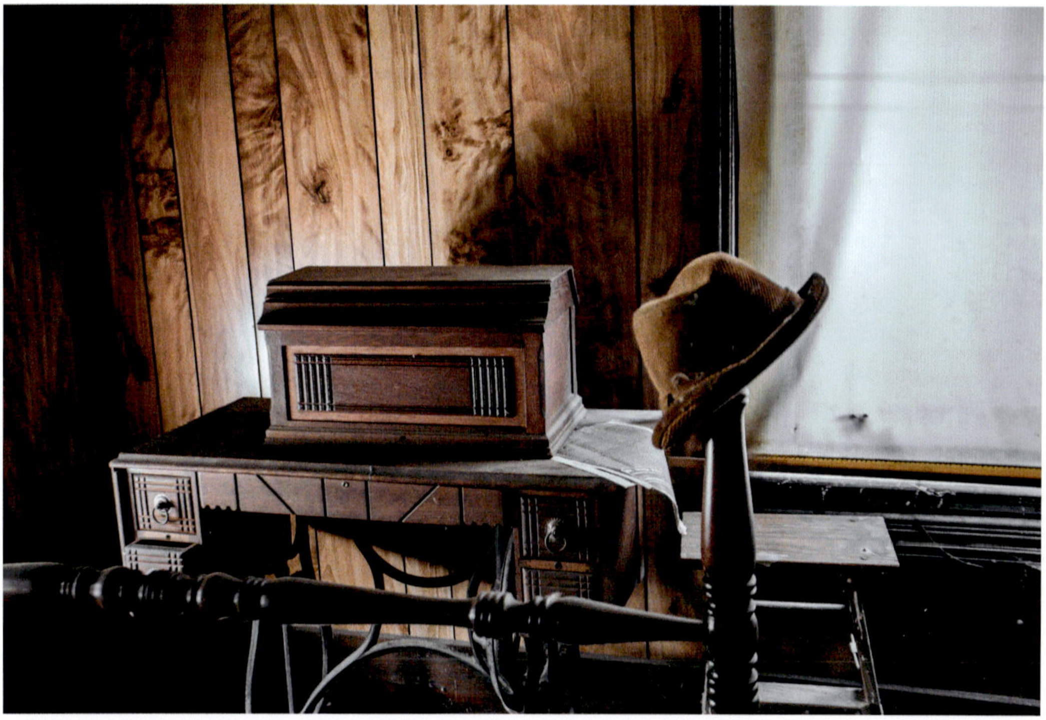

A hat on a bed post is a common sight in southern abandoned homes.

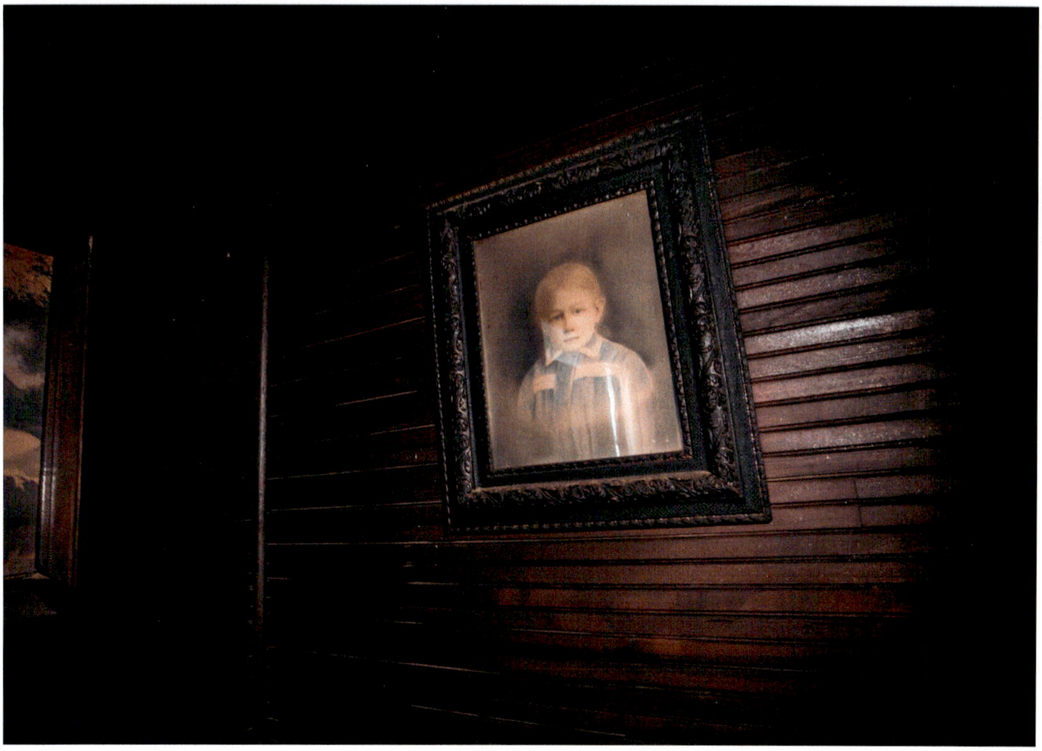

Paintings are still hanging on the walls inside this old home.

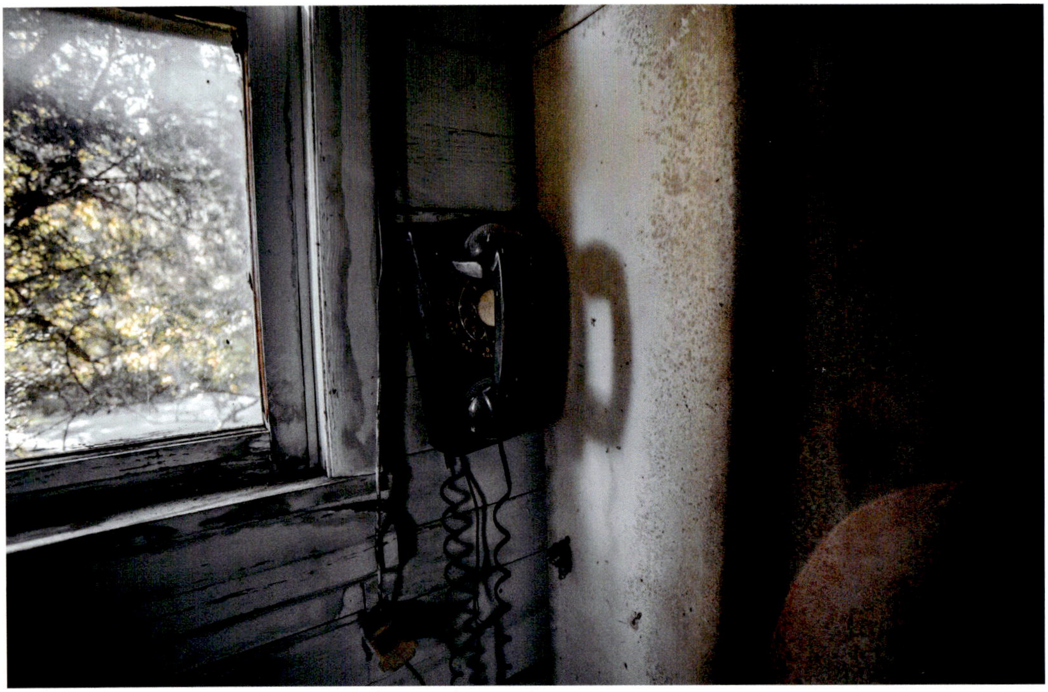

Sometimes these old rotary phones will have the residence phone number on them, usually only four to seven digits long.

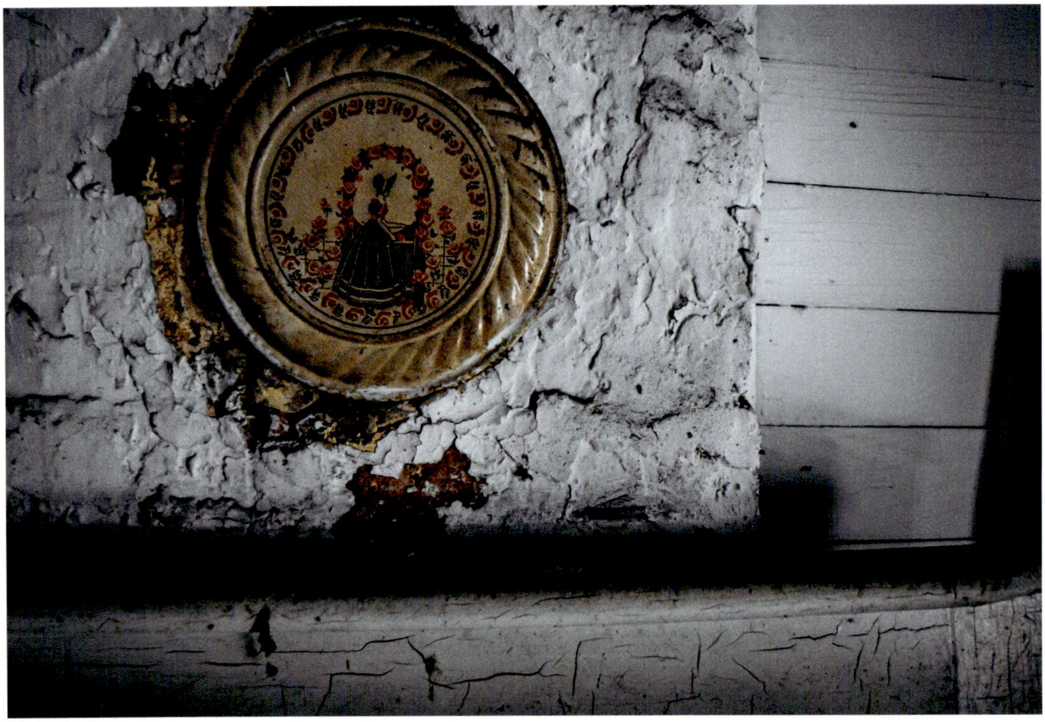

Many older homes used these decorative pipe flume covers for the summer when they removed their heaters until cold weather came back.

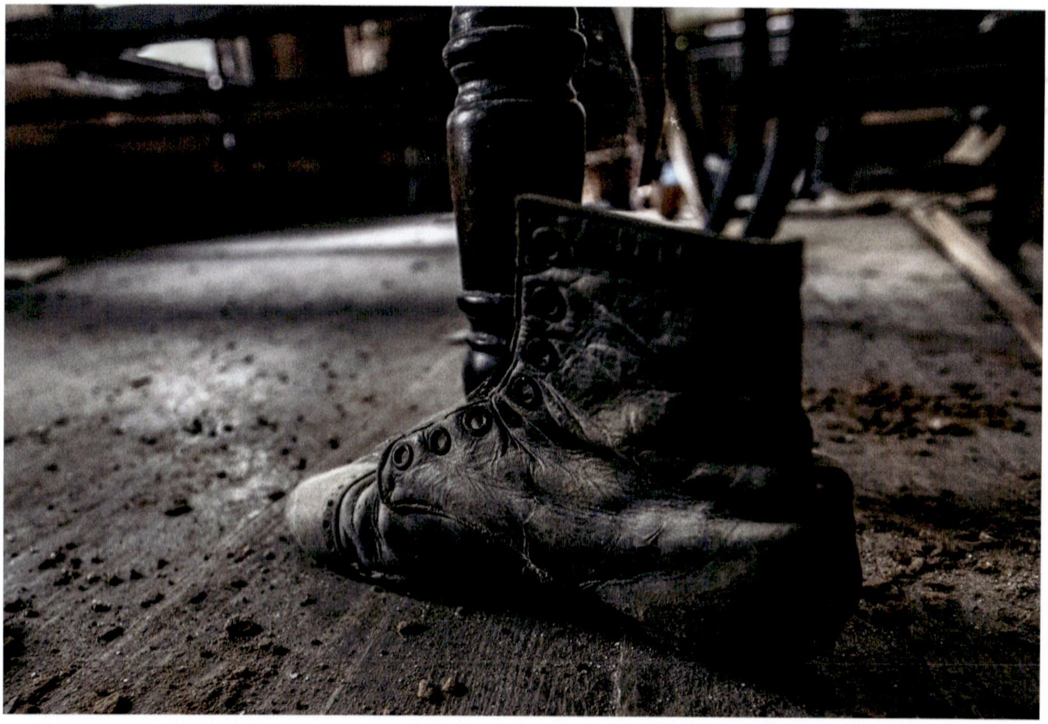

An old boot with years of wear is left behind.

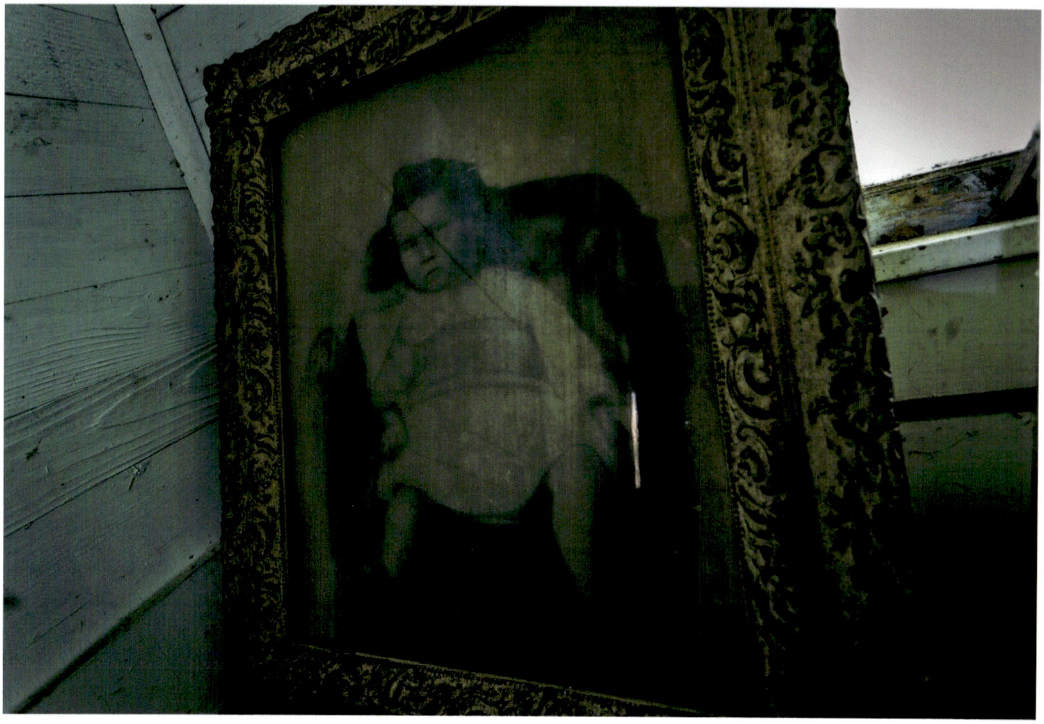

Early portrait photography with unnatural poses and eyes appearing open wider than they are naturally might be unsettling for some.

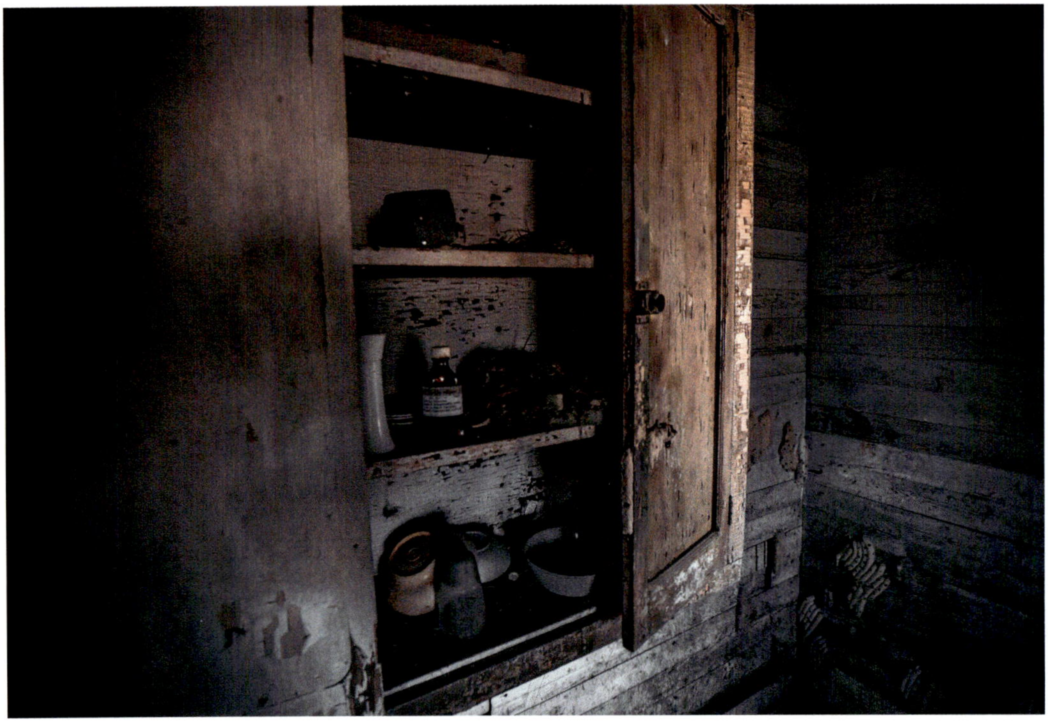

Birds often find their way into abandoned homes and build nests inside cabinets and over doorways.

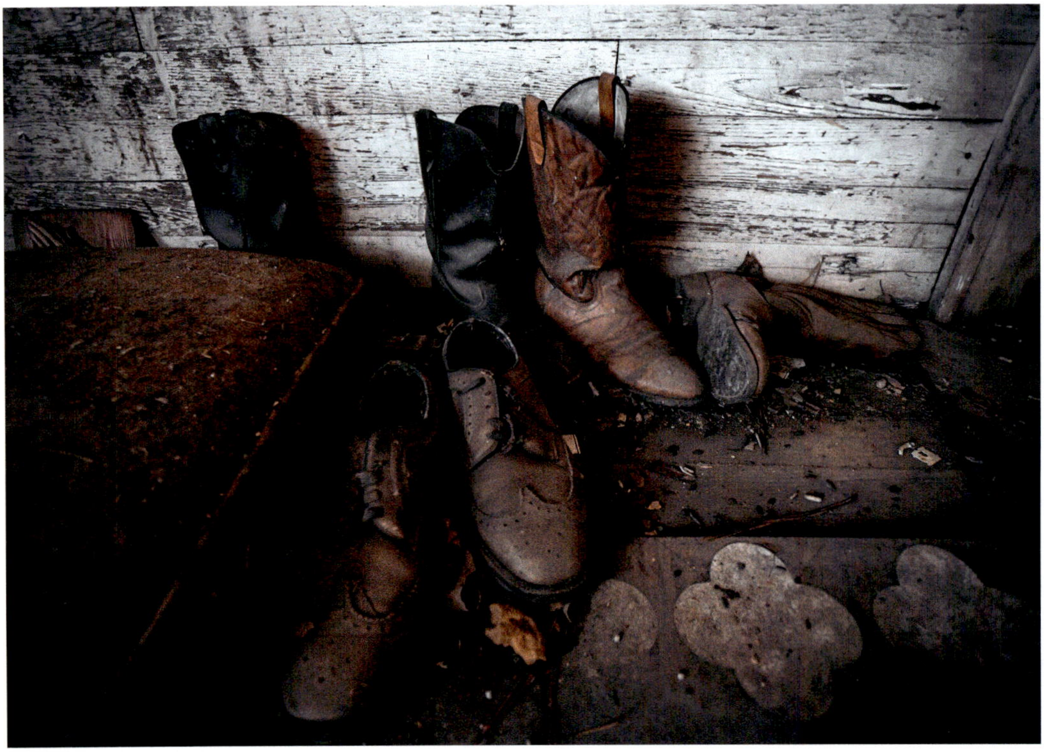

Several pairs of boots still sit against the wall next to the door.

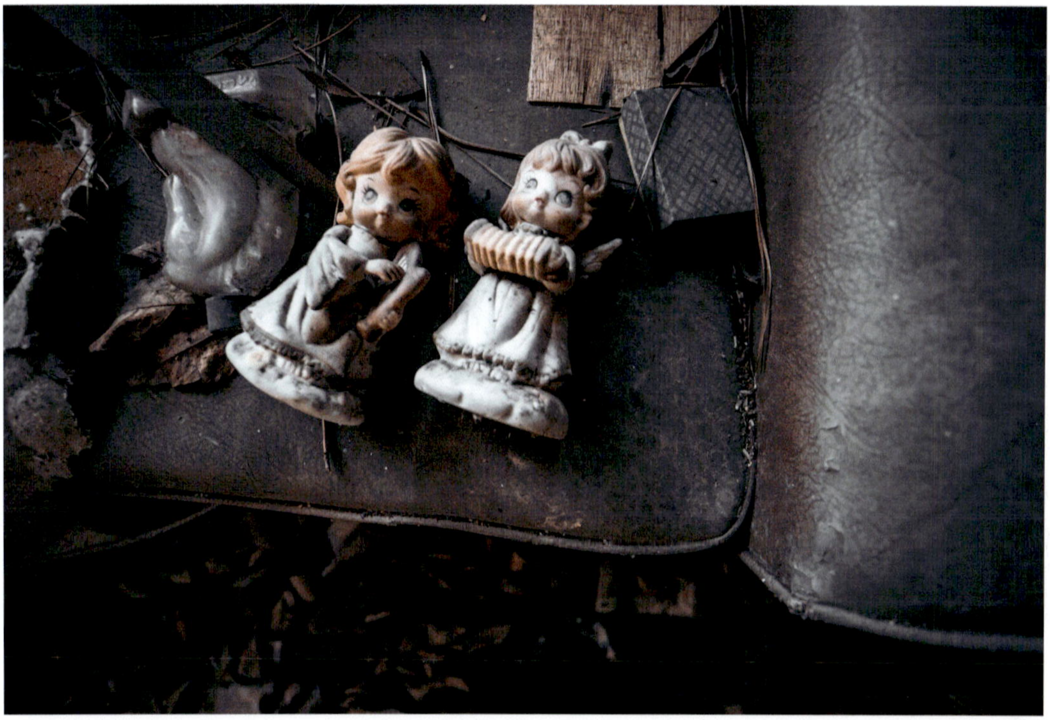

Figurines laid out on the couch still there even though a collapsed roof has exposed them to outside elements.

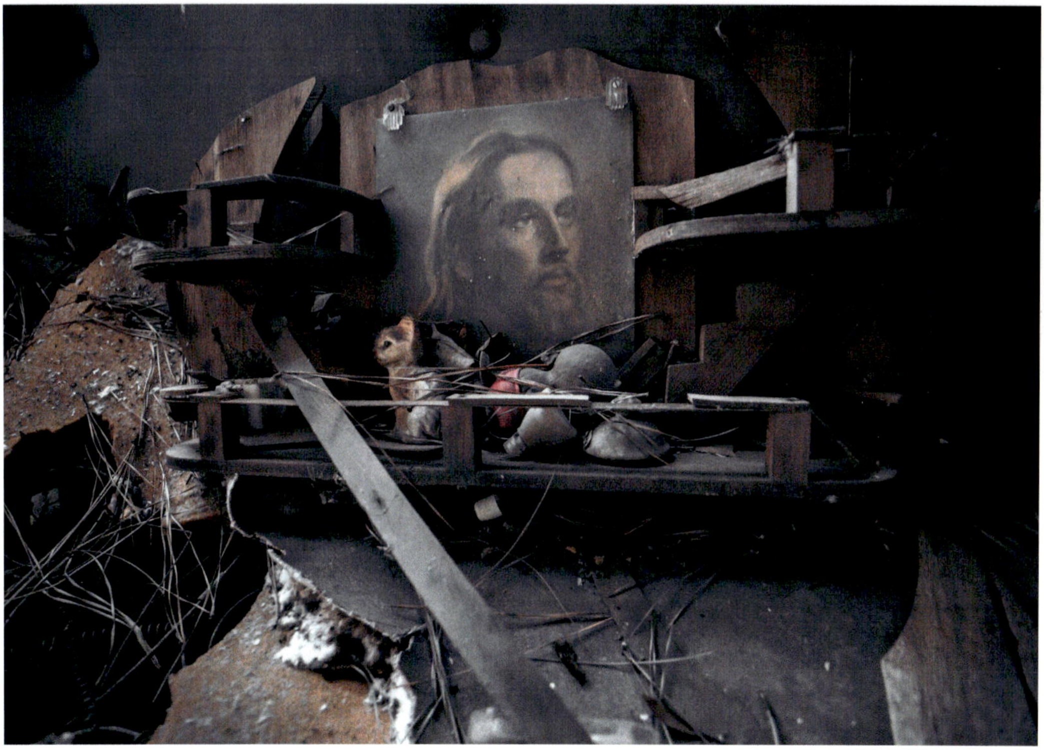

A picture of Jesus still hanging on the wall despite everything falling around it.

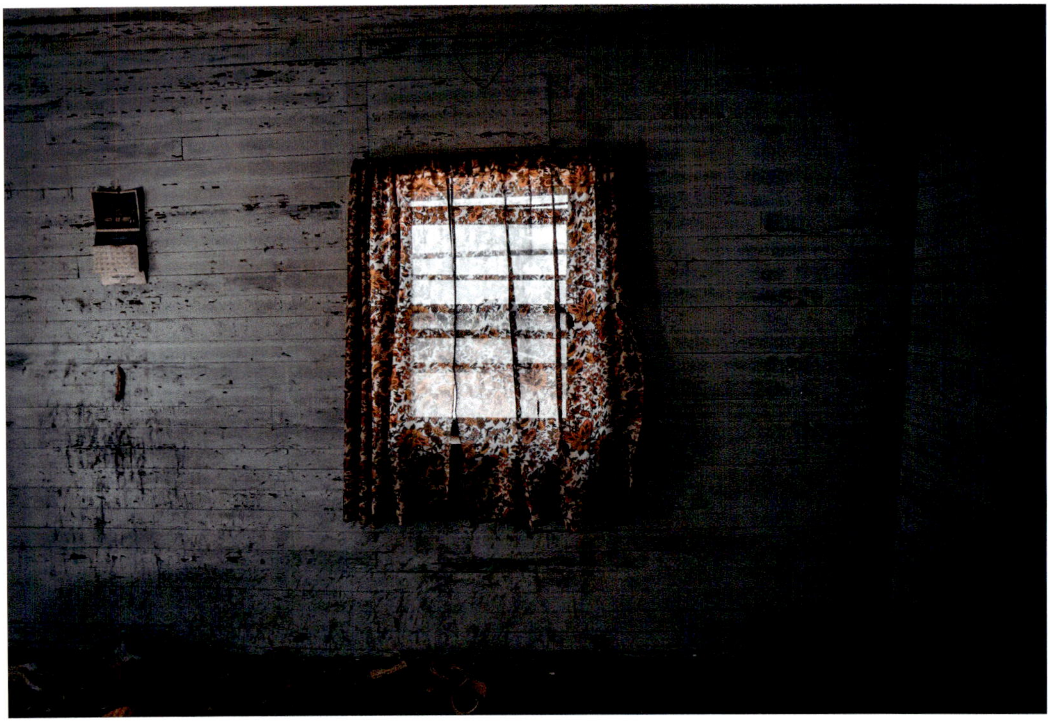

It seems like even when there is not floral wallpaper in the old southern homes, you can at least find floral curtains.

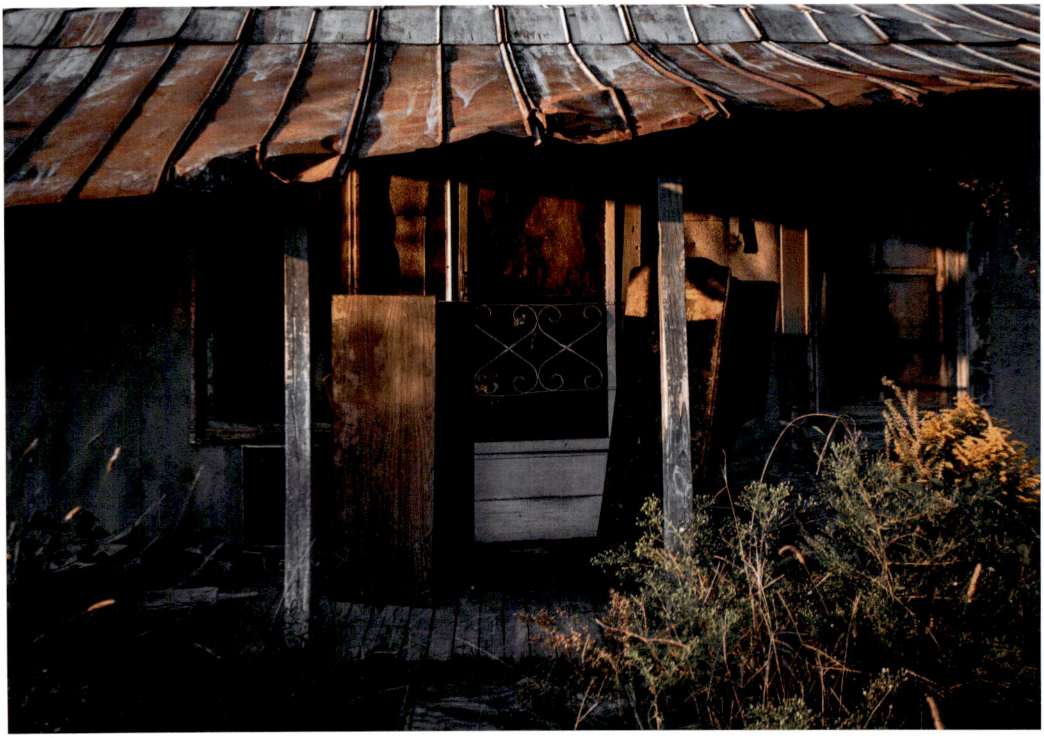

The front porch of an abandoned one-bedroom home.

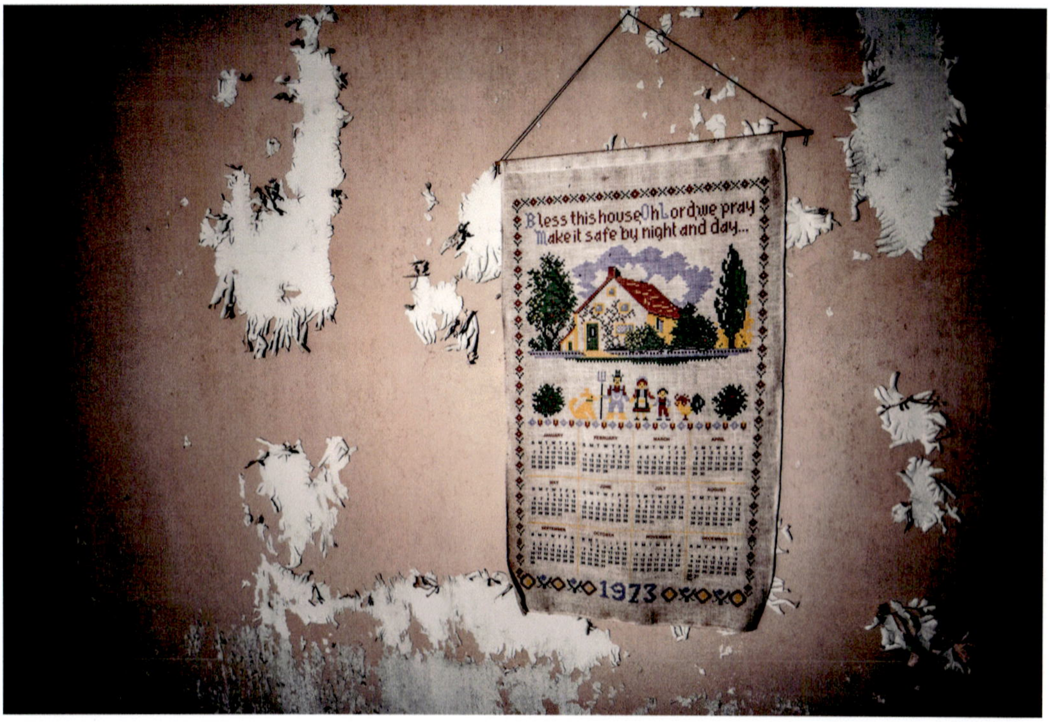

Calendars still hanging on the wall are usually a good hint for when the home was last lived in.

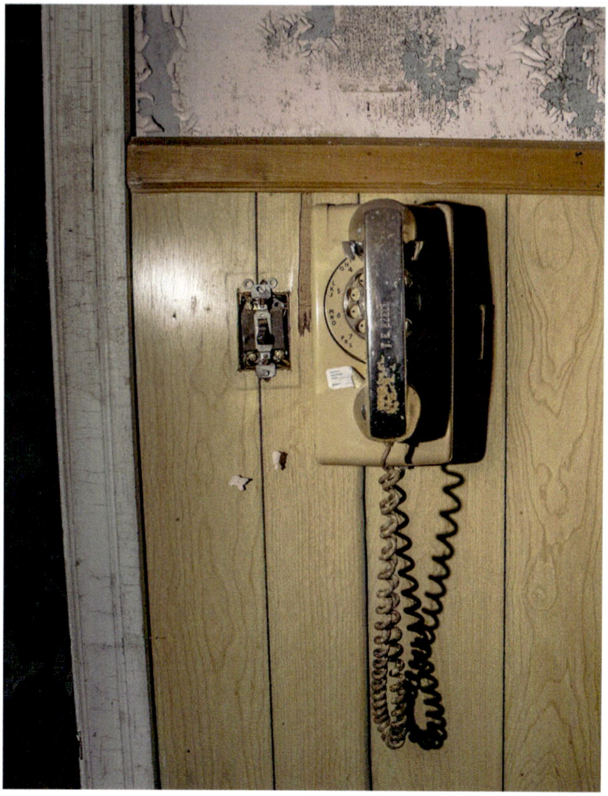

Another old rotary phone still attached to the wall in a residence that was abandoned likely in the late 1970s.

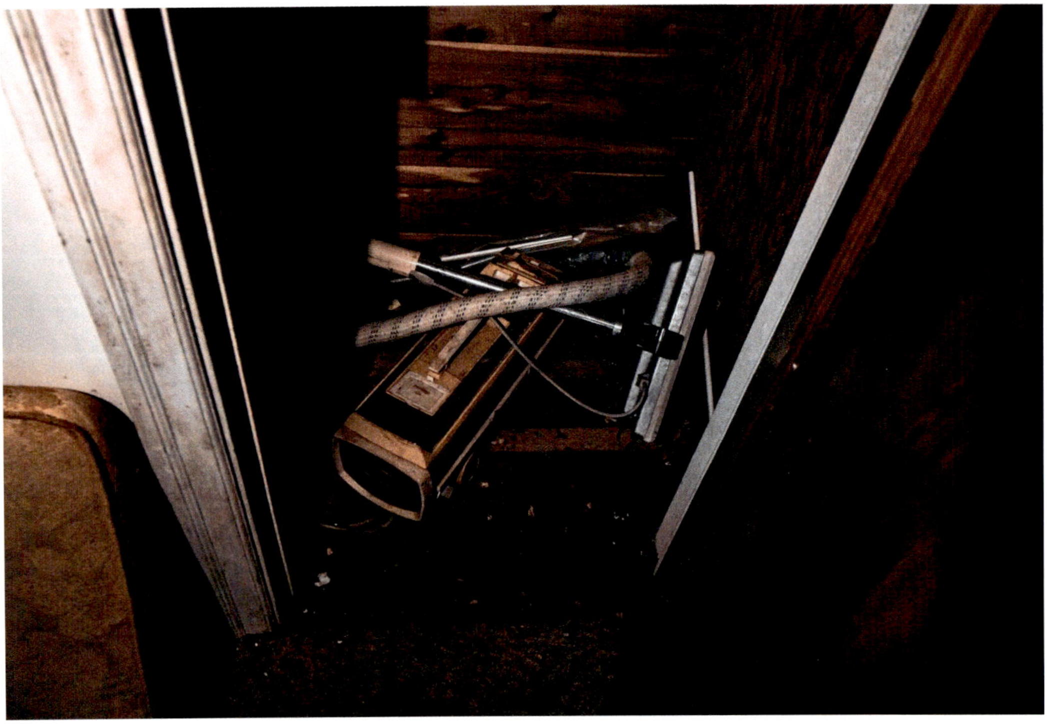

An old vacuum cleaner and all of its accessories still sit in one of the mostly empty closets.

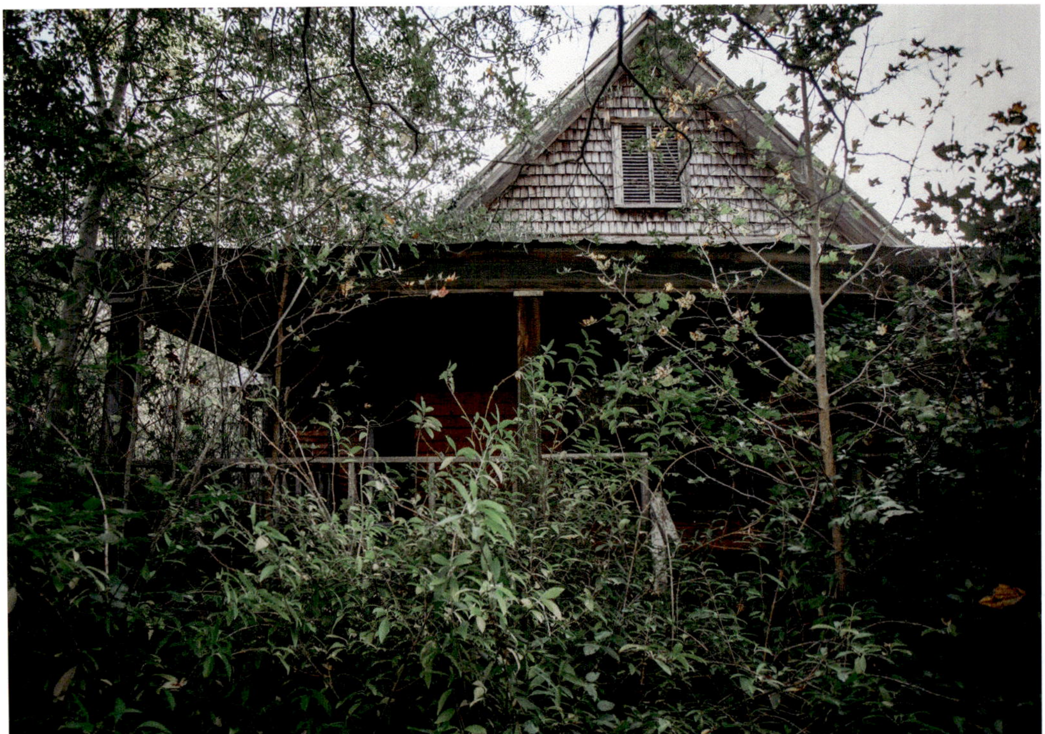

Another house covered by brush is no longer visible from the road.

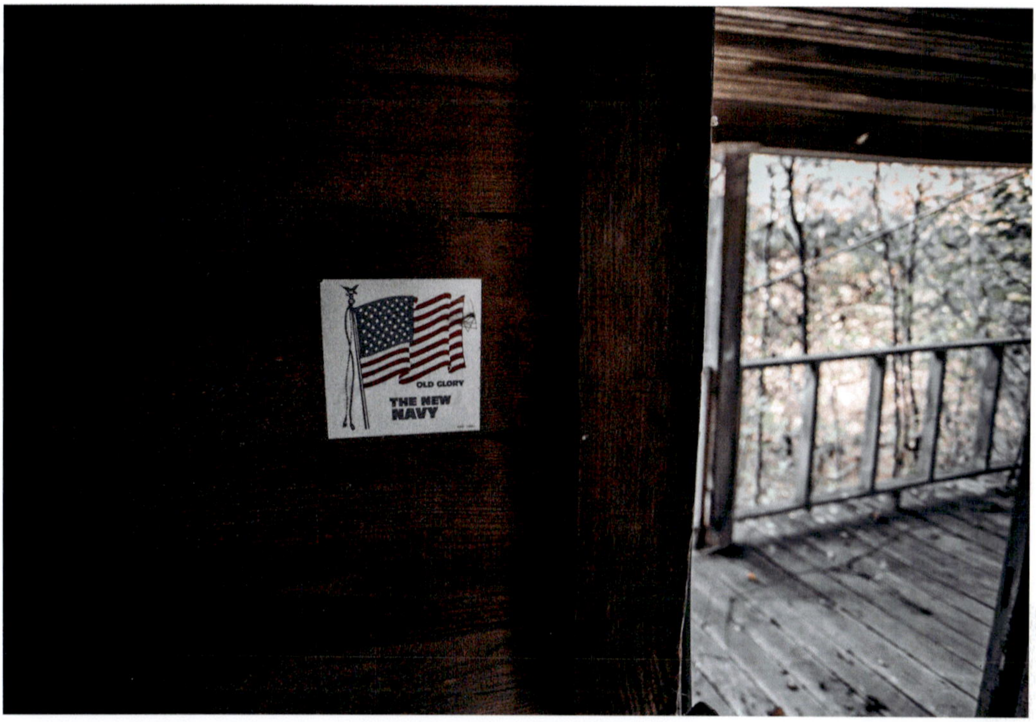

One thing you can always count on in old Southern homes is a large amount of patriotic and religious décor.

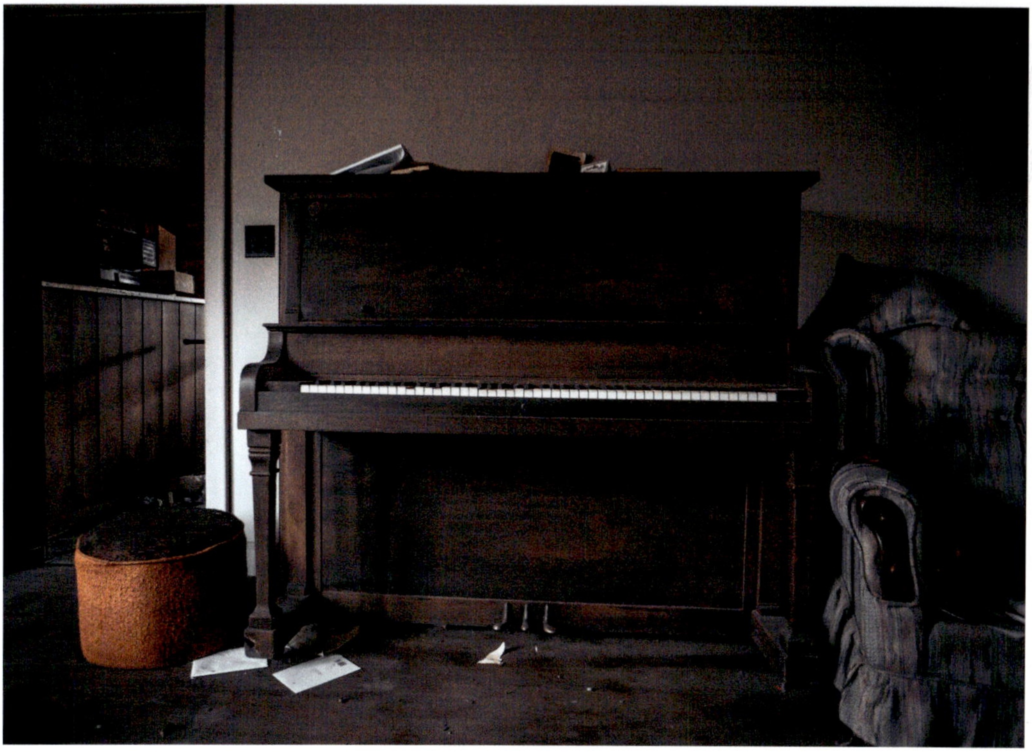

Another house where the piano is the center of the family's living space.

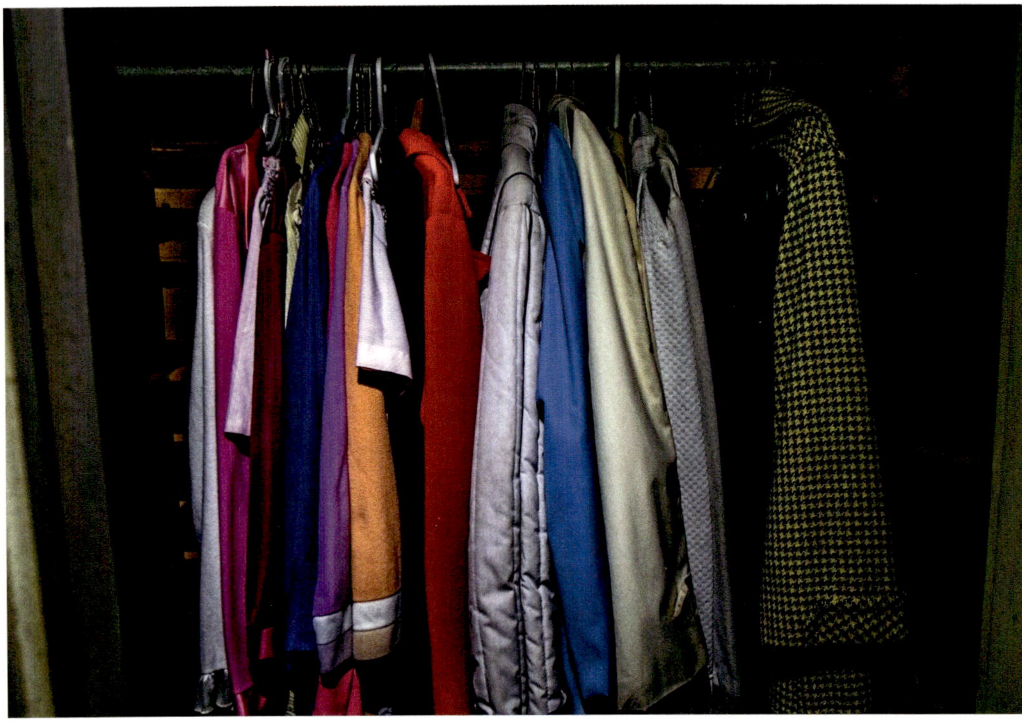

It is always exciting to see what clothing is left behind.

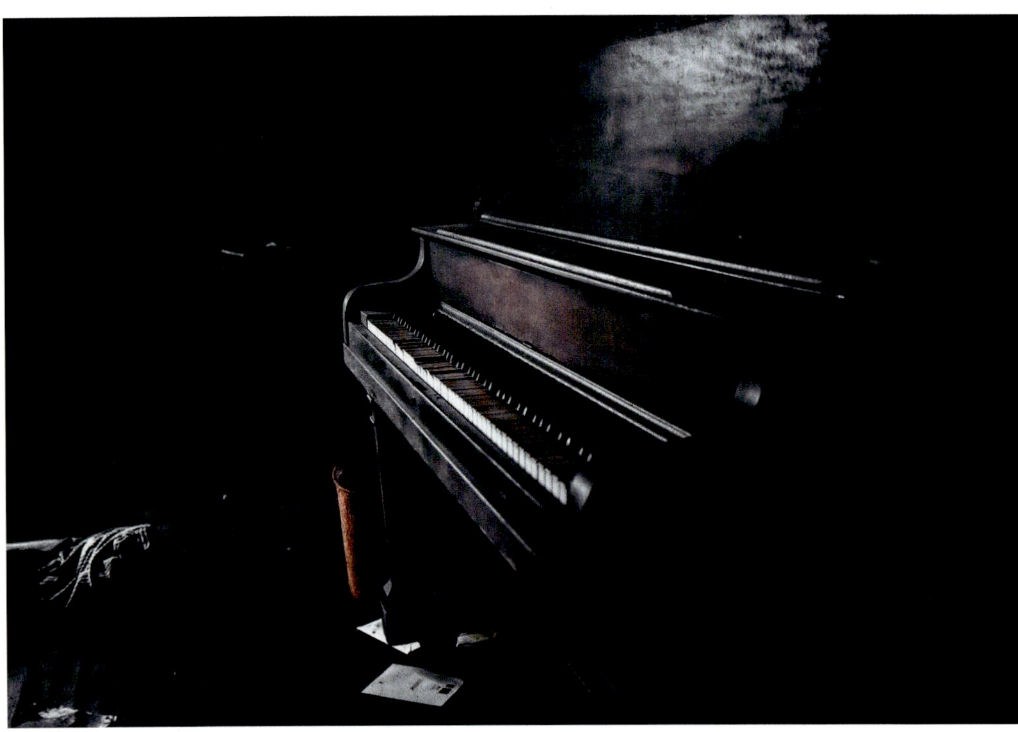

There is a joke among urban explorers about pianos always being left behind due to their weight and size.

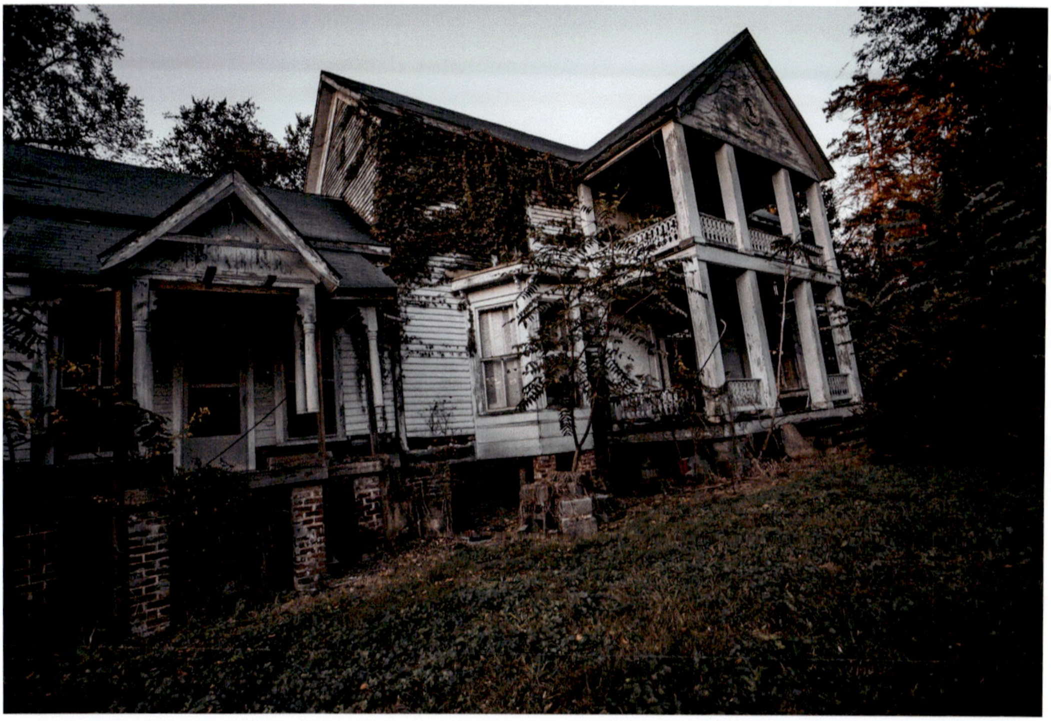

While photographing this house, we were told that small house attached was where slaves lived when the house was first built.

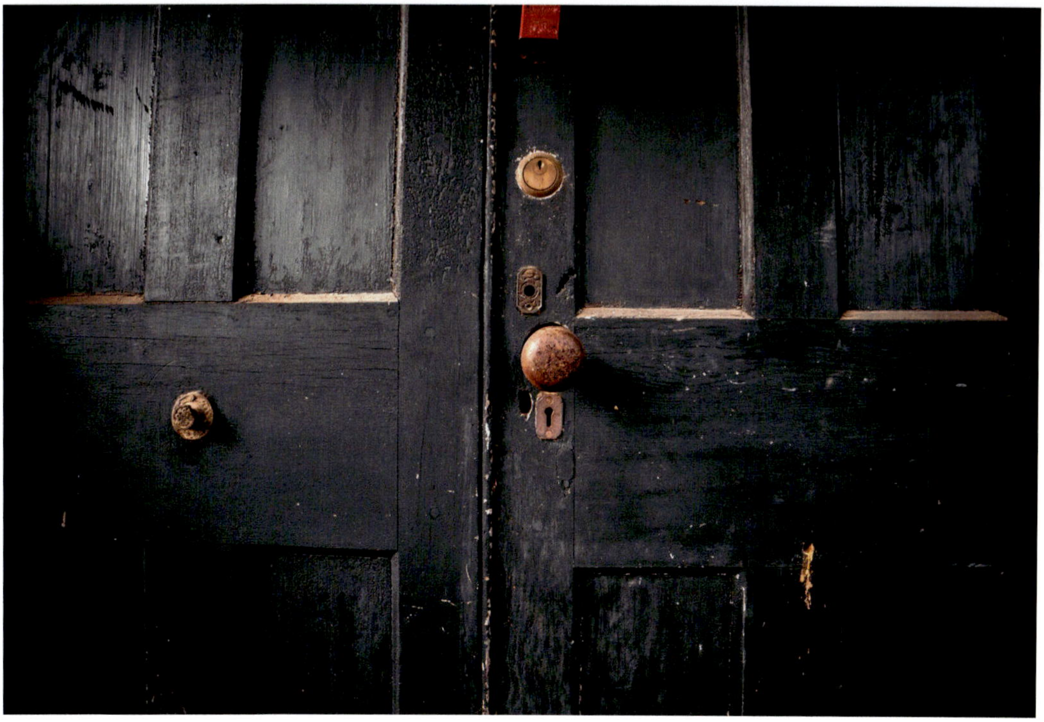

This particular door has been through many different types of locks since the home was built.

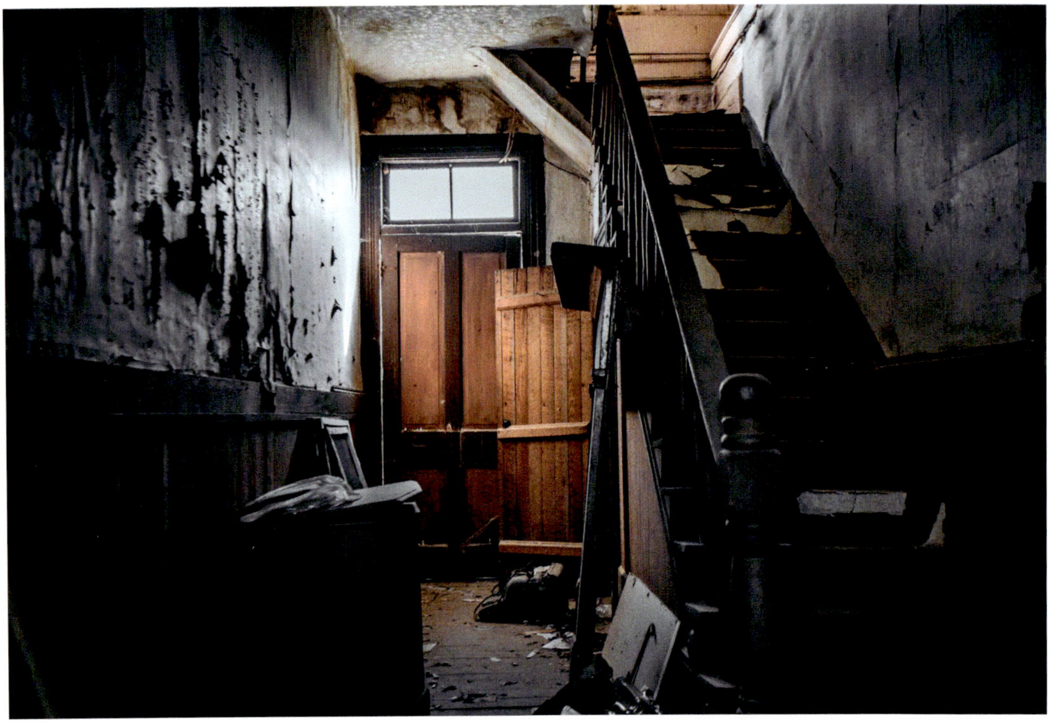

Time and negligence are beginning to take their toll on this beautiful stairwell.

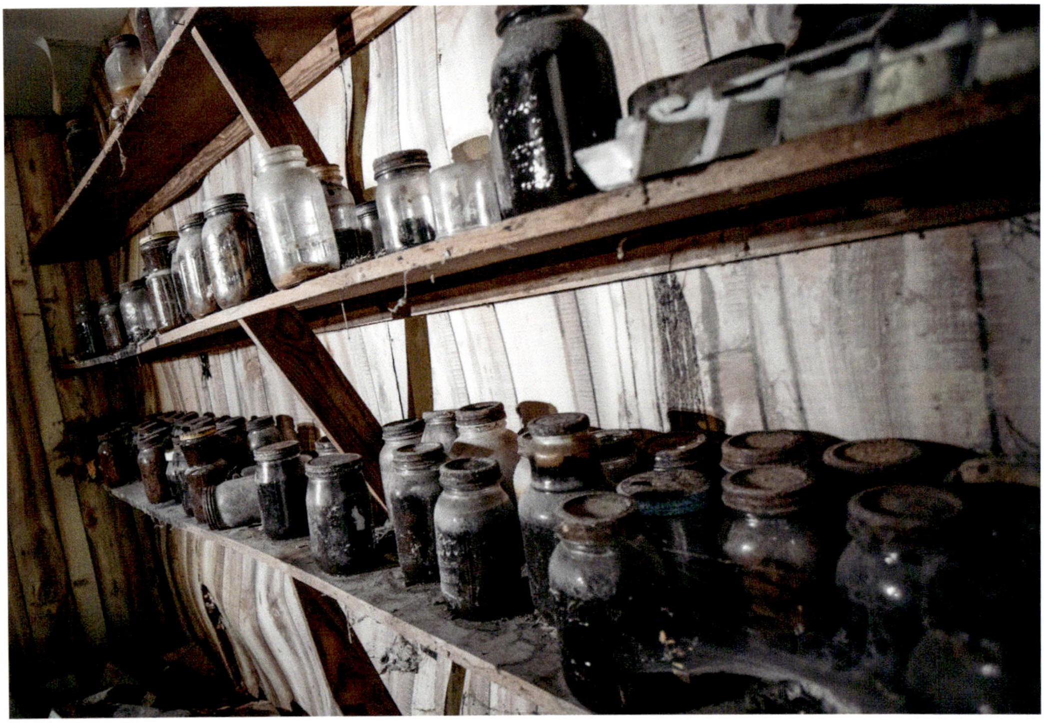

Canning was a convenient way for people to store foods for long periods of time, but these have sat on these shelves for well past their intended timeframe.

9

WHAT'S LEFT?

You go down enough backroads and you are sure to find places like the ones I have featured in this book. It would take a lot more ink and paper to show you everything I wish that I could show you. I have reserved this space for the strange, unexplainable, and the awesome that did not quite fit in previous chapters.

Items shrouded in mystery can sometimes be revealed in the strangest ways. I became friends with someone without knowing she had lived in one of the houses I had explored. I mentioned travelling through her hometown when she told me that her childhood home was abandoned. She began to describe it and immediately I knew which one it was. This house had always been strange to me because I remembered toys being in the kitchen cabinets, so I asked her. She told me that when her parents were upset with her, they would take away the toys and store them in places she could not reach.

I always find it eerie when an item of significant value is left behind. I have seen jewelry and shoes worth a small fortune, cars that could easily be sold and rebuilt. I found an intriguing wooden-framed radio in a house once that I could not stop thinking about. I looked it up and it was a rare model that was selling online for thousands of dollars. A fan I posted a picture of got a lot of attention online and a friend messaged me and let me know he had just spent hundreds of dollars on the exact same model.

While looking for the story in one house, my daughter stumbled upon something that seems so far removed from today that she stood there in shock; a Ku Klux Klan membership card with the homeowner's name and member number printed boldly on the front. While it may seem like something only connected to us through distant ancestors, people still walk around who saw this area during a time when racism was not only common but encouraged. Finding this was almost surreal even for someone who grew up in a place that was once so deeply rooted in racial injustice. That item that still sits in a decaying home in North Alabama is a direct link to a not so far removed past filled with civil atrocities.

Whether these were items of value, emotional or monetary, they sit in limbo. Will these pictures be the last they are seen or heard of, or will they once again become a part of someone's life? I know a doll in one of these pictures now sits underneath the weight of a church building that finally gave in to the forces pushing it back into the earth. I wonder if in the building's 130 years on this planet standing tall and facilitating thousands of people who came there to worship, if I was the last person to lay eyes on the inside. Was I where its story ended?

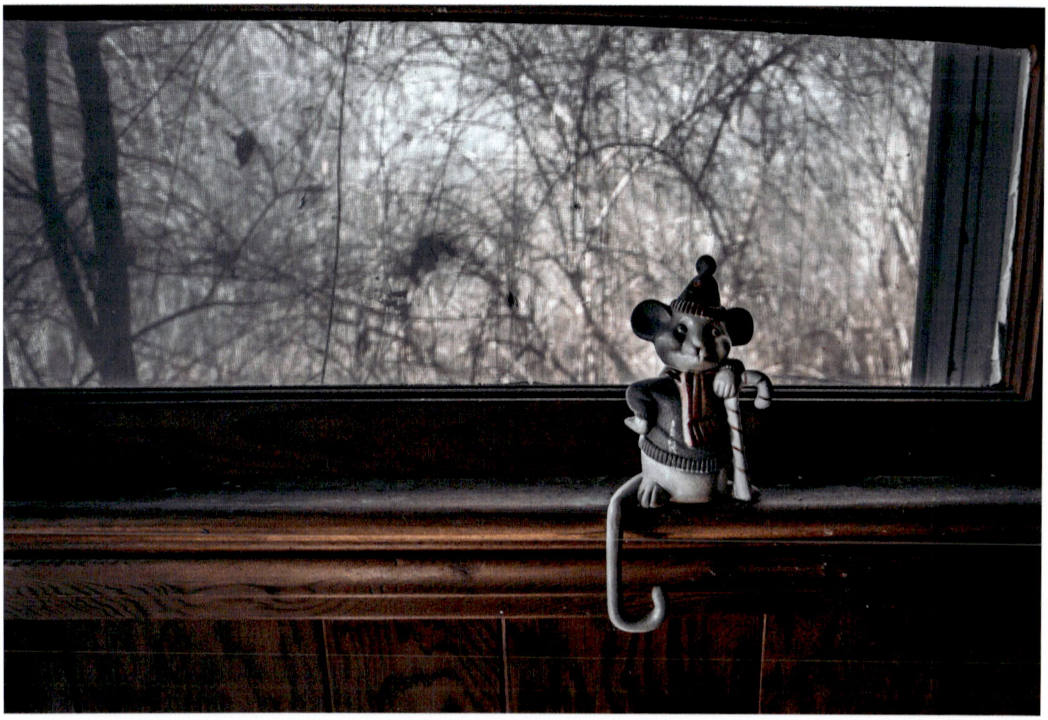

A decorative toy still sits in the window long after the house is left behind.

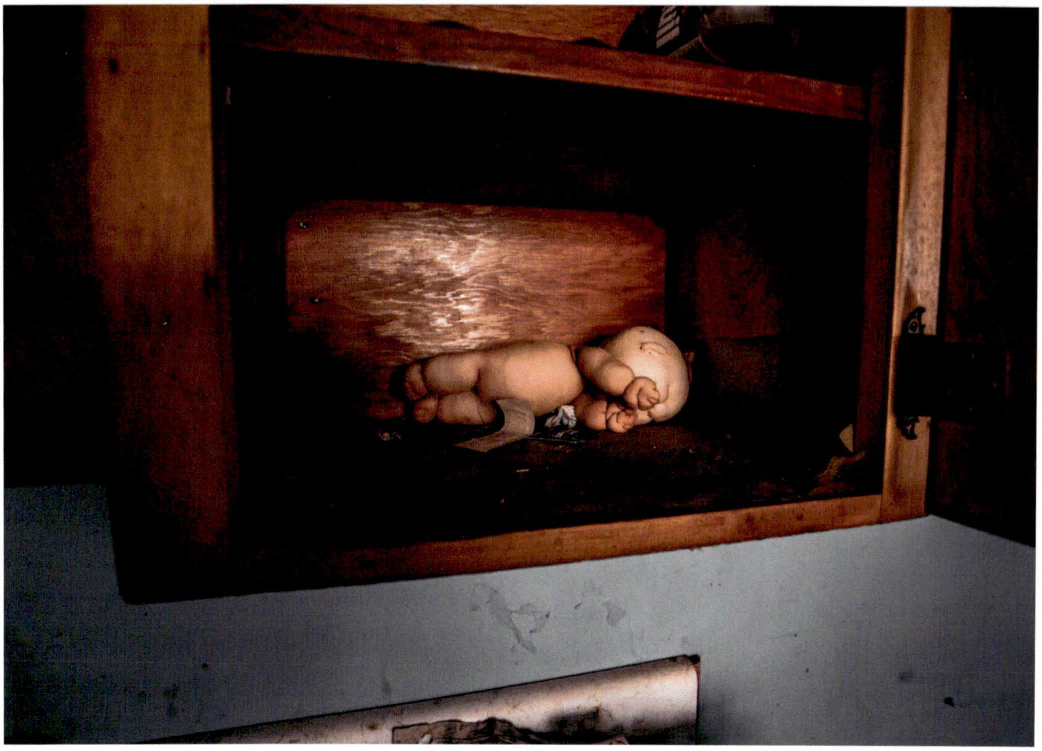

A toy inside a kitchen cabinet.

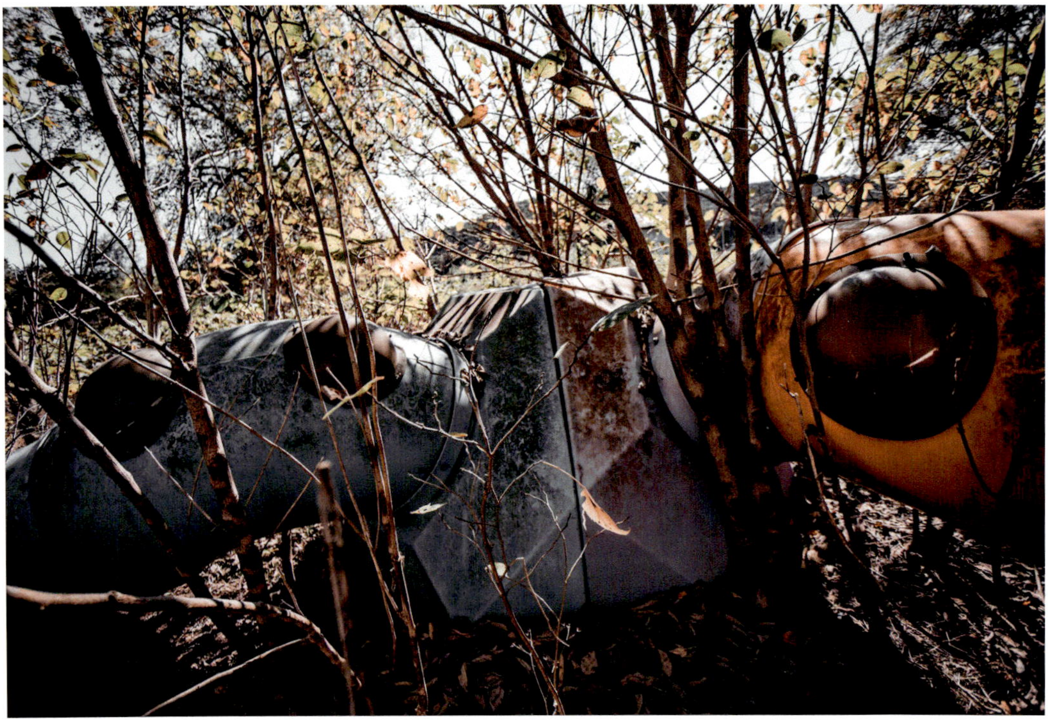

This house had a playground from a popular fast-food restaurant behind it.

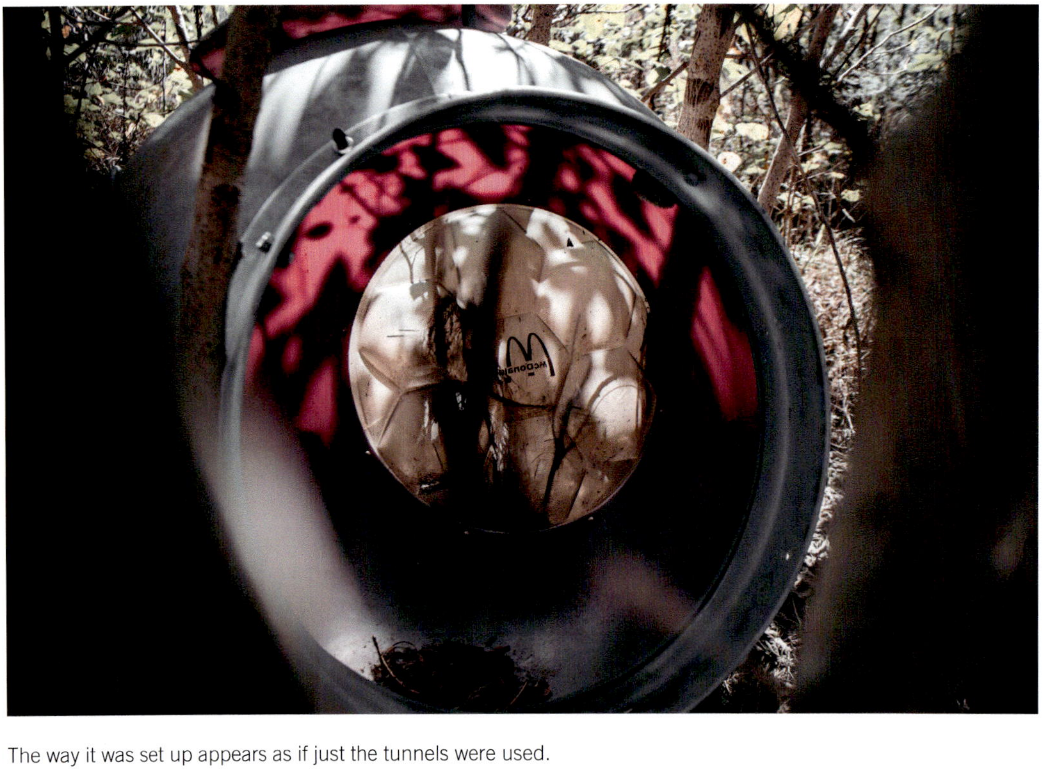

The way it was set up appears as if just the tunnels were used.

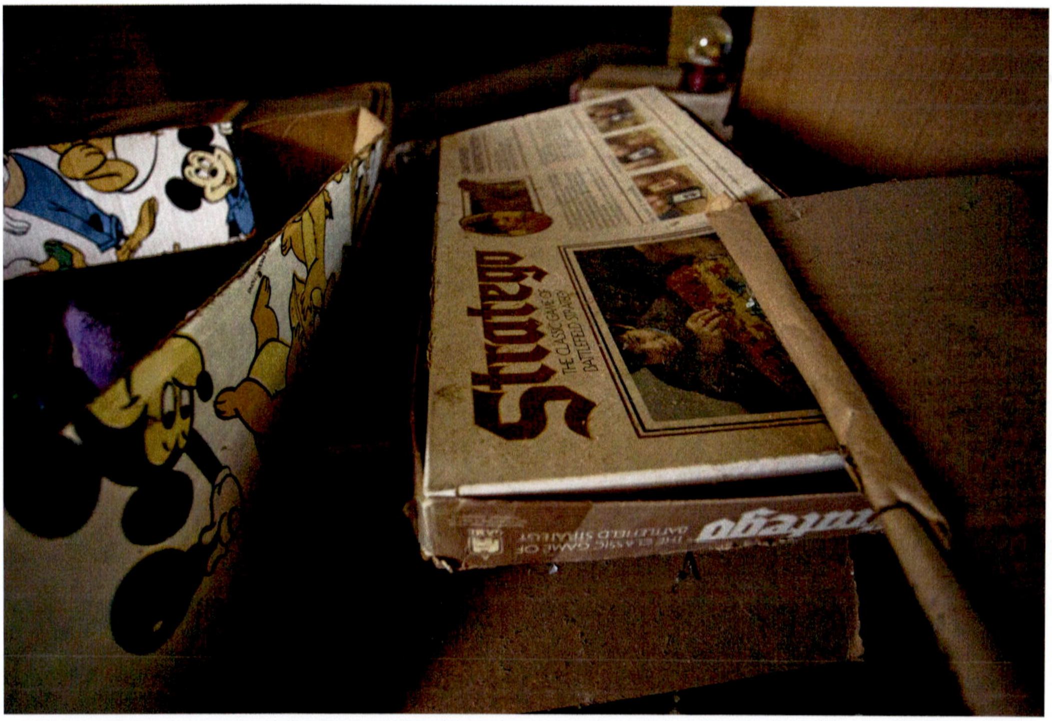

Vintage versions of board games that are still popular are a common sight.

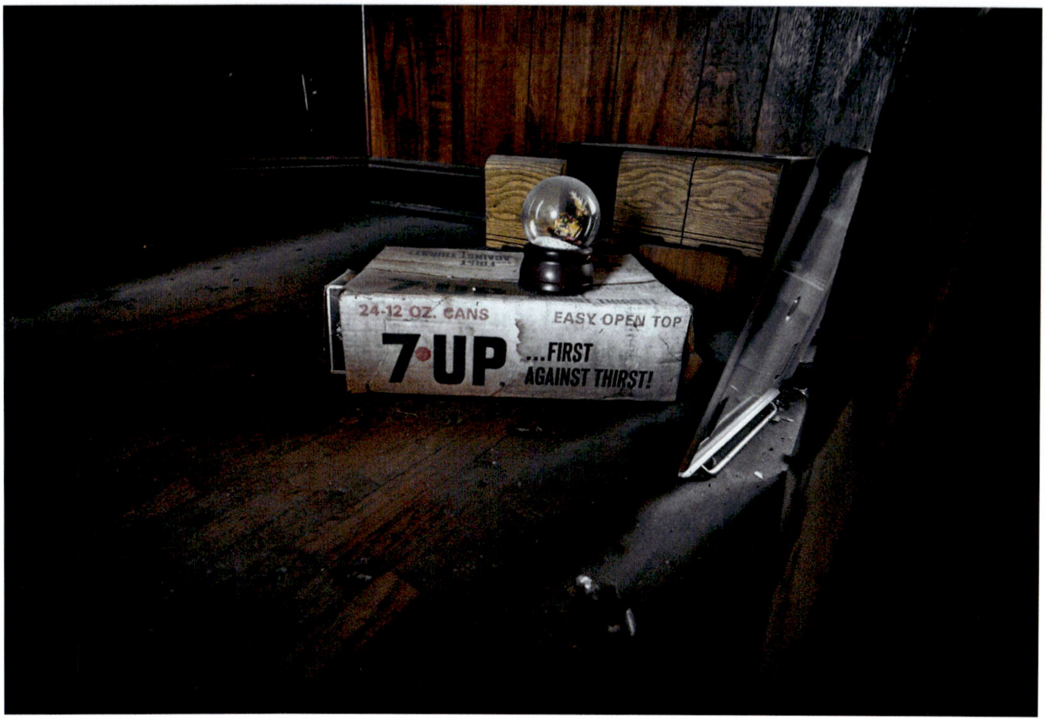

Soda and other popular products can be dated quickly by the slogans used as most companies have updated them multiple times.

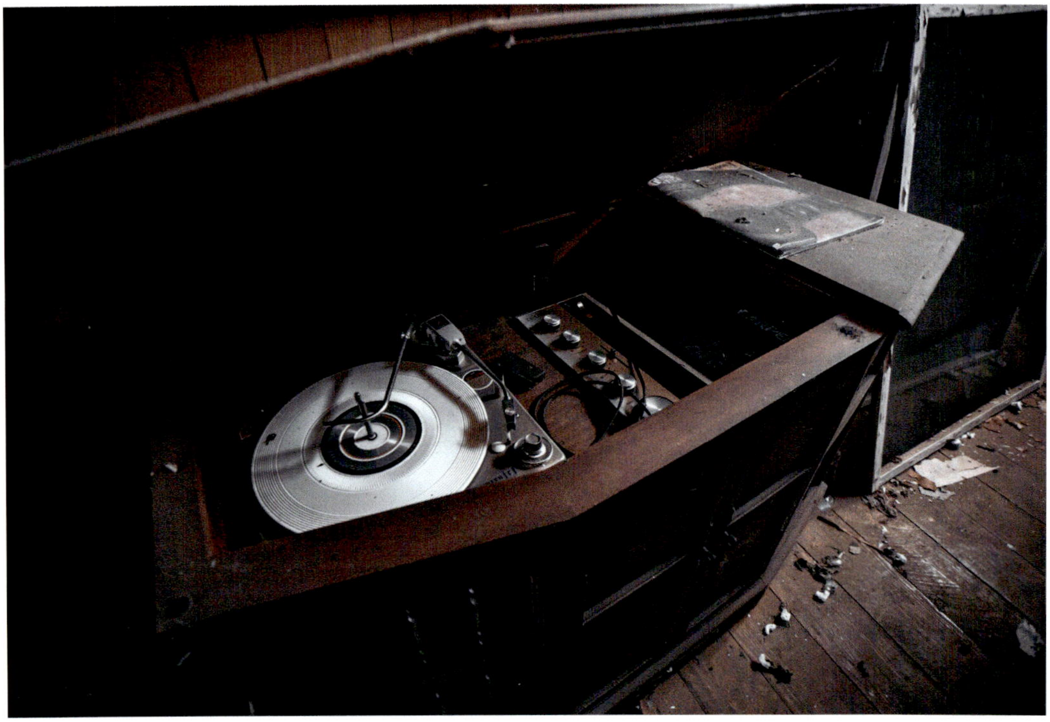

An old record player sits in an abandoned house despite the recent popularity of vinyl records.

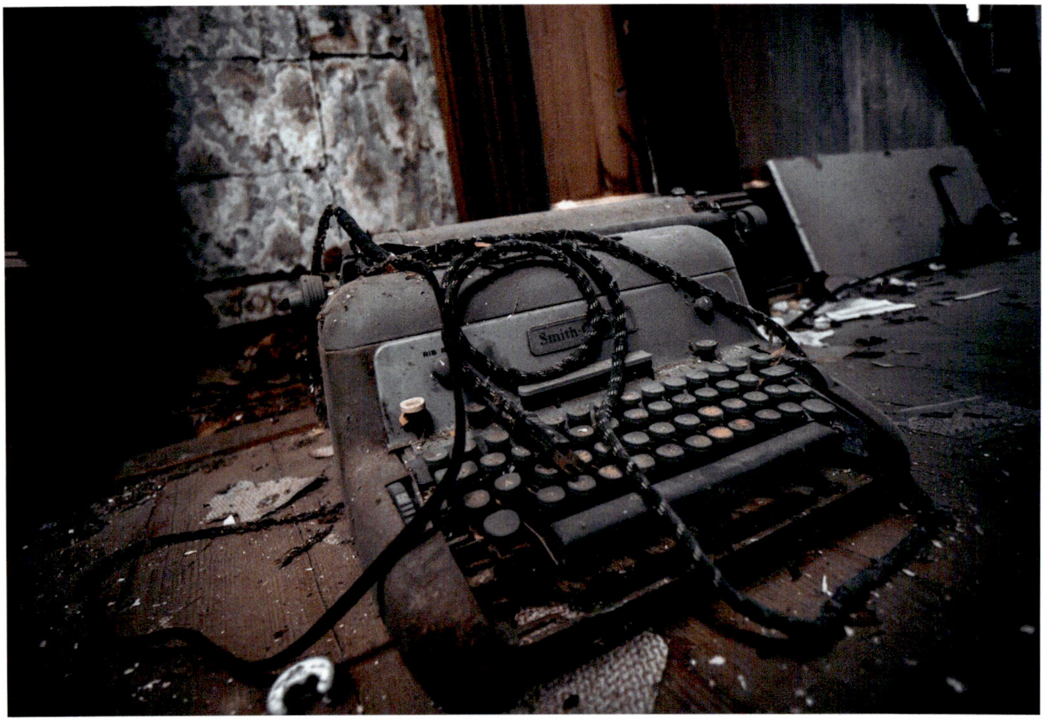

Typewriters are another common find in these abandoned homes. The forgotten technology that was left behind still holds value in the hearts of people who have used it.

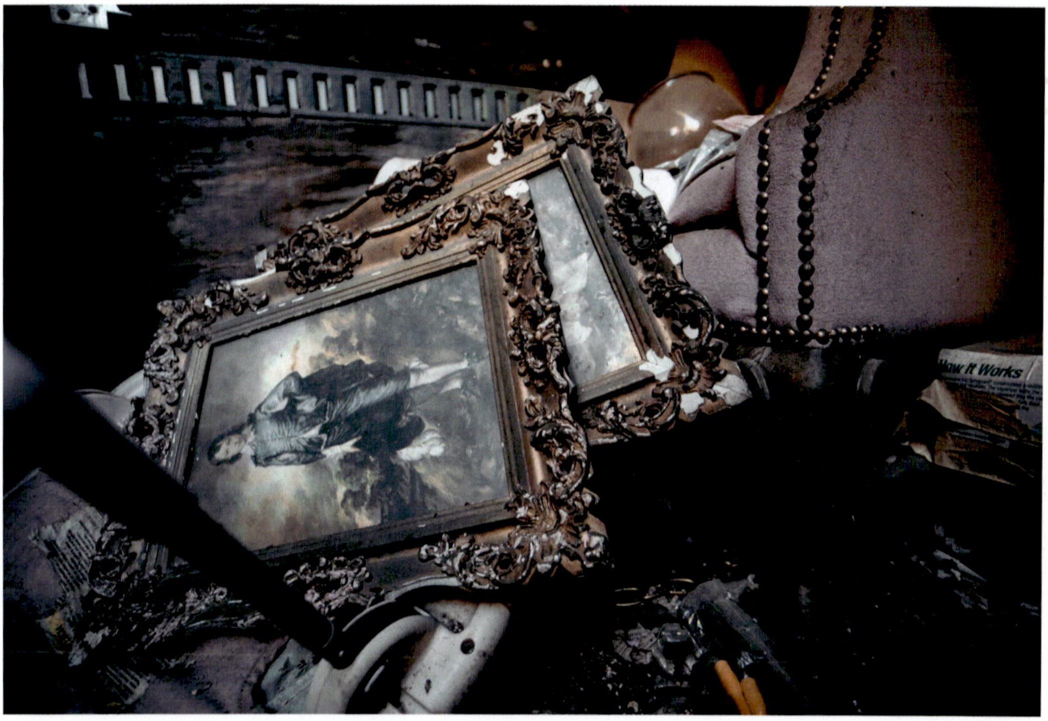

Intricately framed art sits in a storage trailer behind an old house.

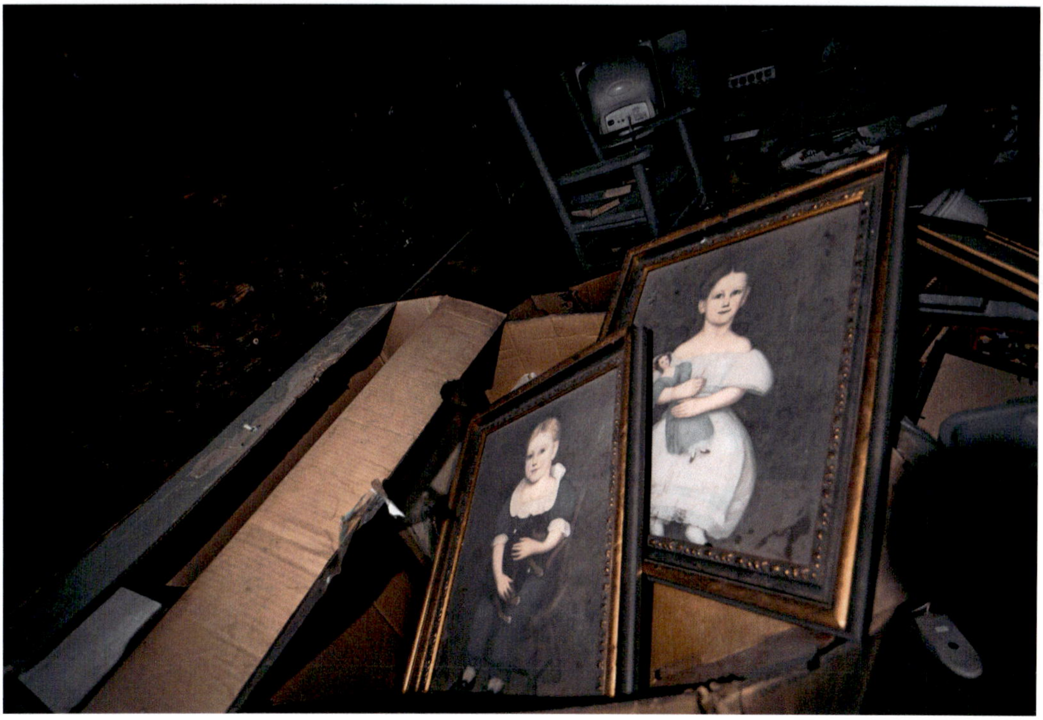

Painted portraits were a way of capturing memories of loved ones before photography was widely used.

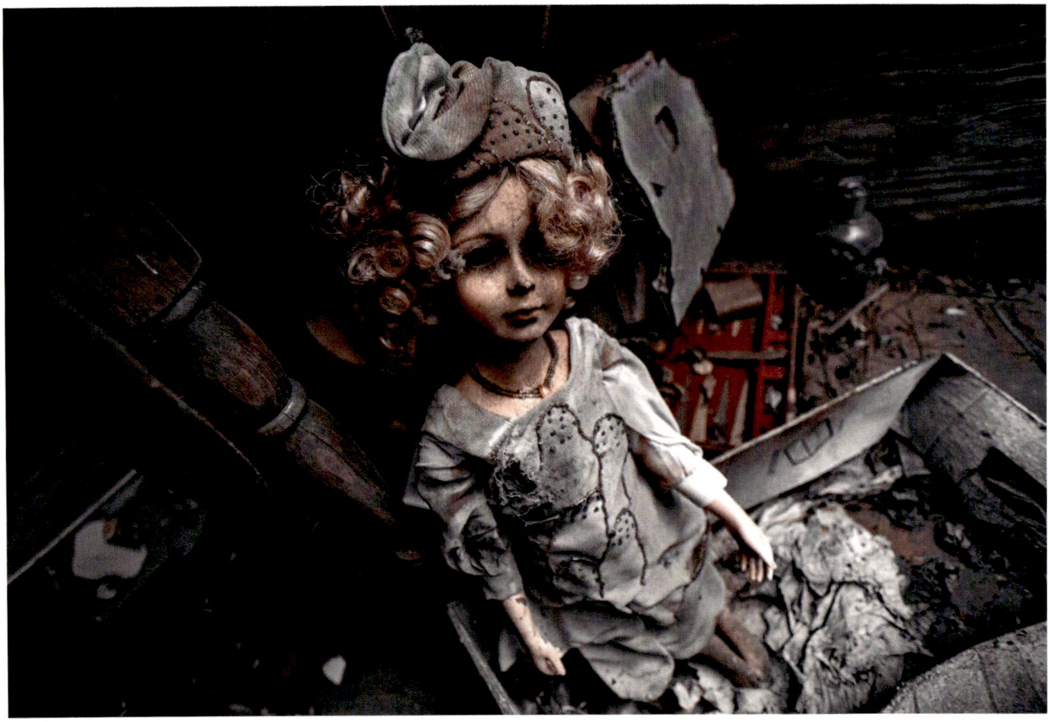

A beautifully crafted old doll sits in the storage trailer.

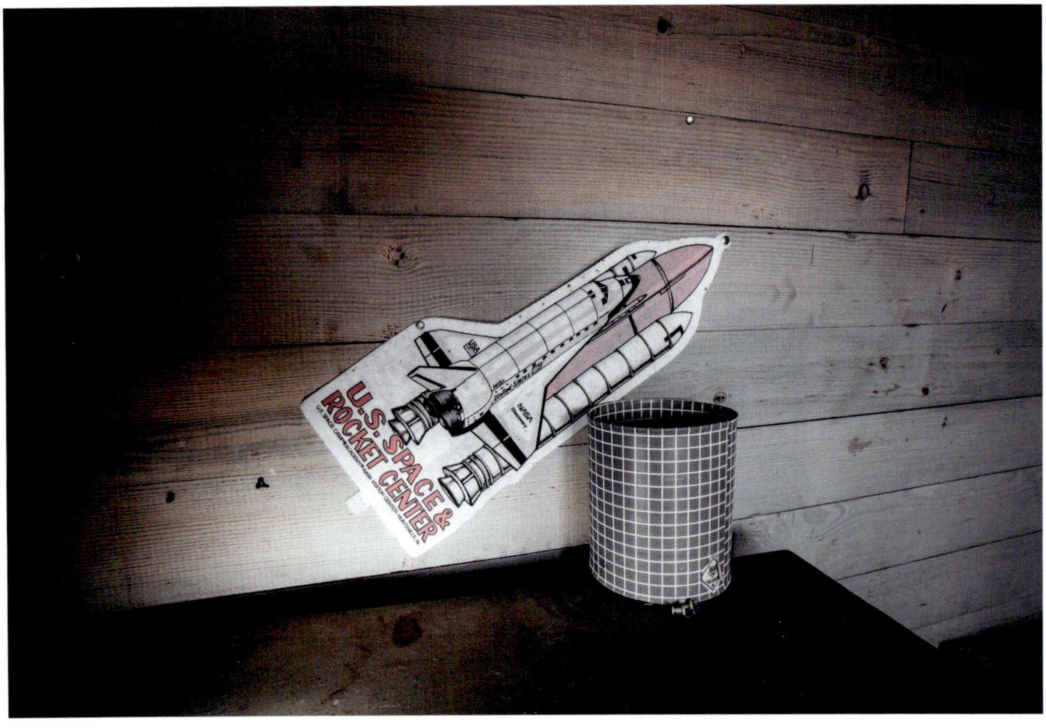

North Alabama's relationship with space exploration has apparently been celebrated in the homes of its residents for many years.

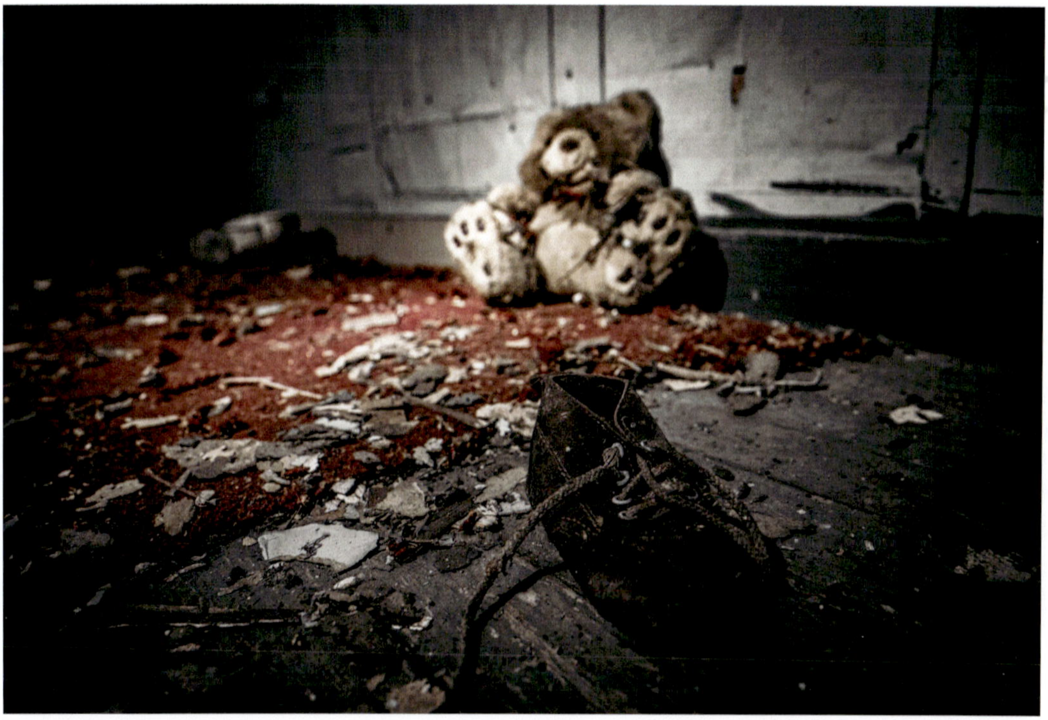

An old shoe and a teddy bear are all that are left behind in this old dog-trot style home.

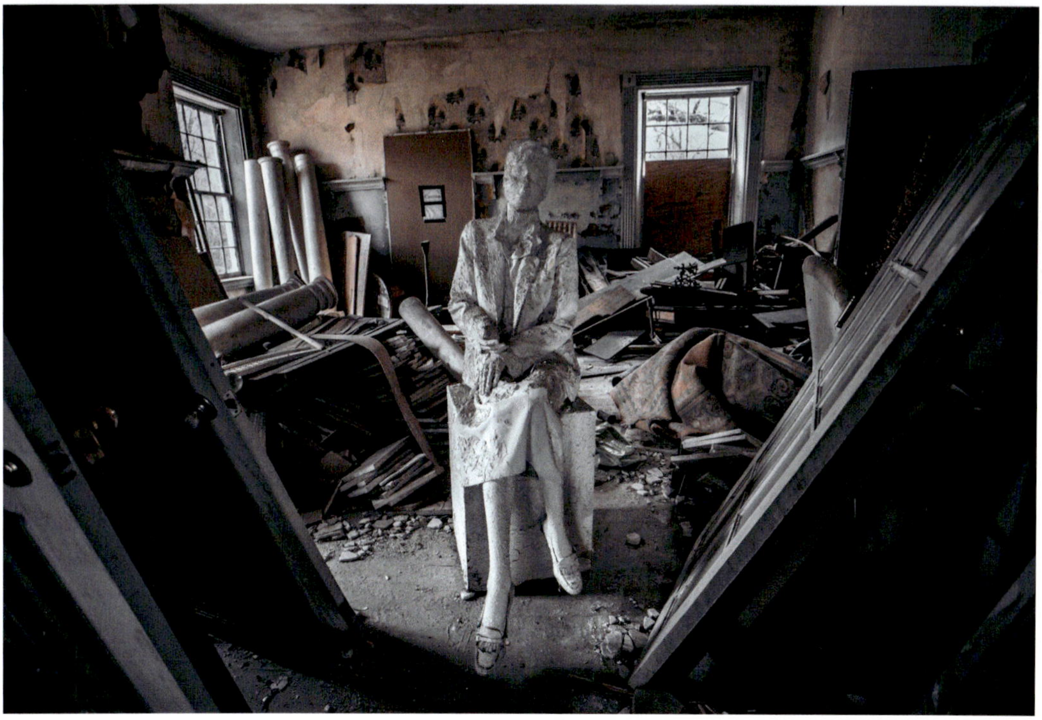

A plaster statue left behind in a historic old North Alabama home.

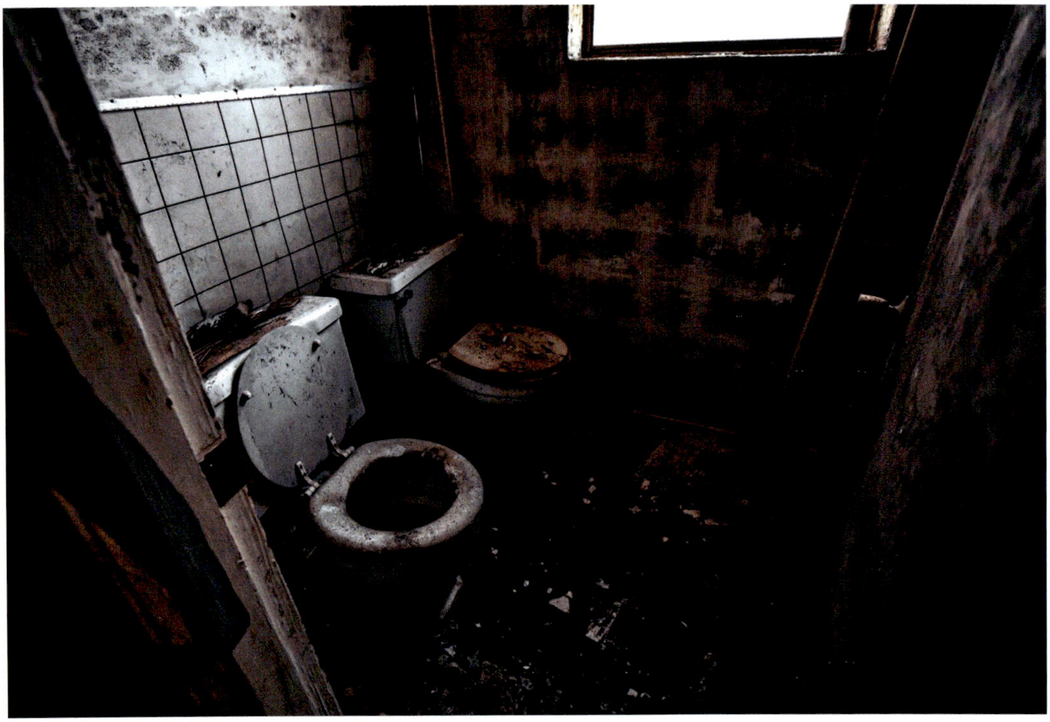

When the stall falls off the wall, a public restroom gives a very strange aura.

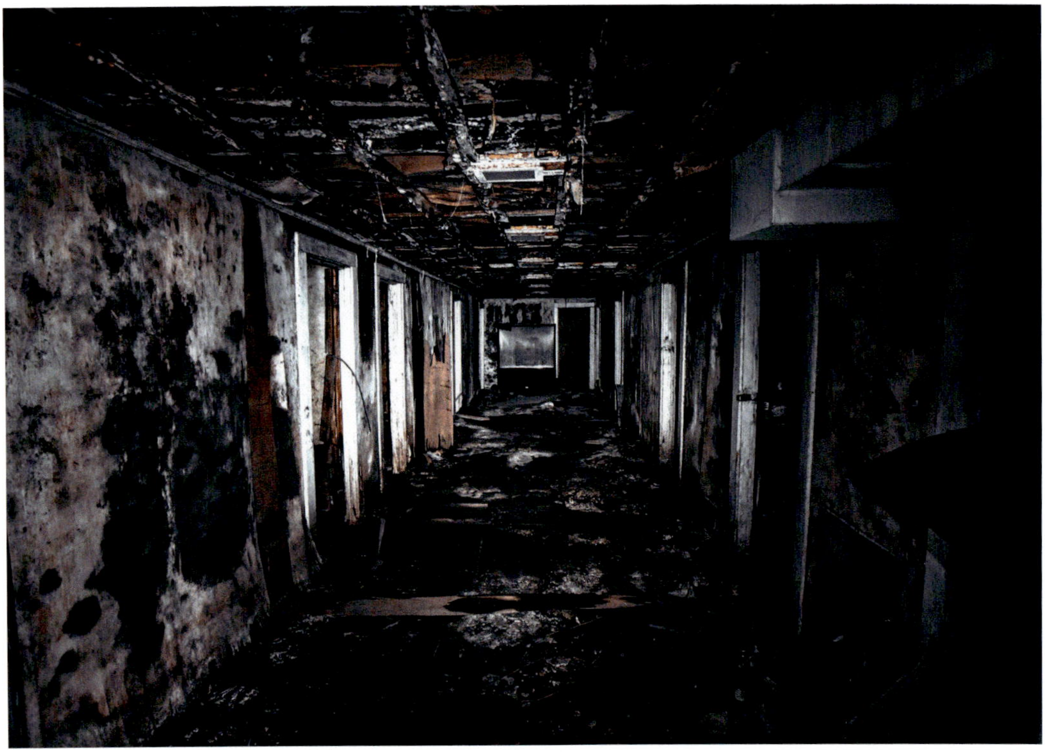

Extensive water damage and black mold make this church basement resemble something out of a horror movie.

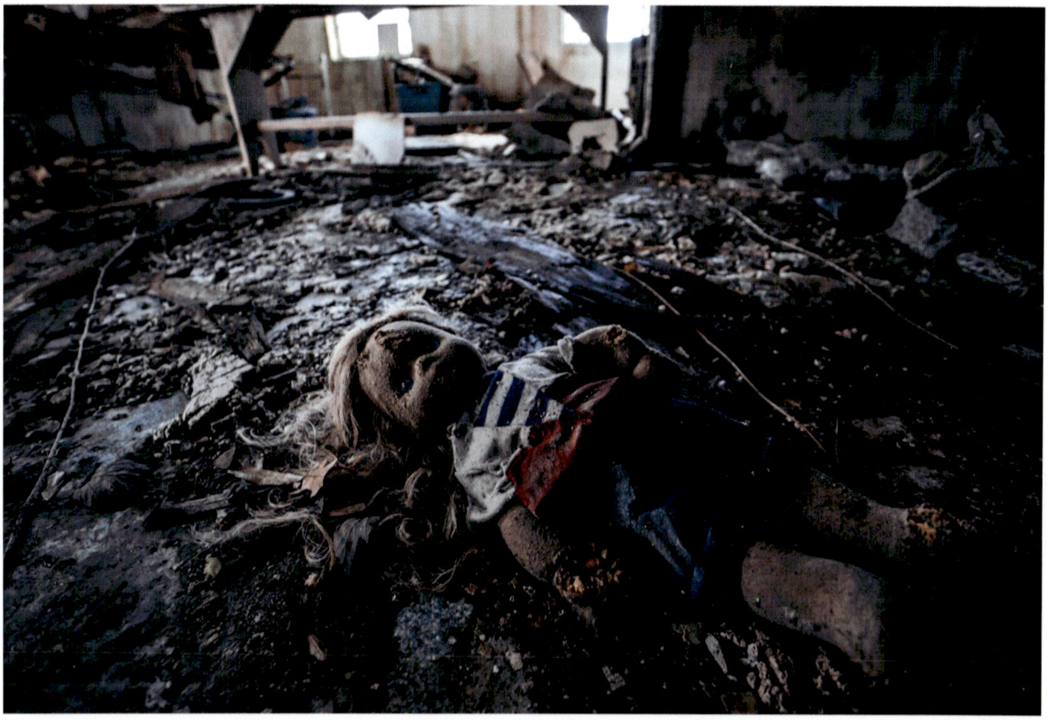

A doll that now lies underneath the weight of a collapsed church.

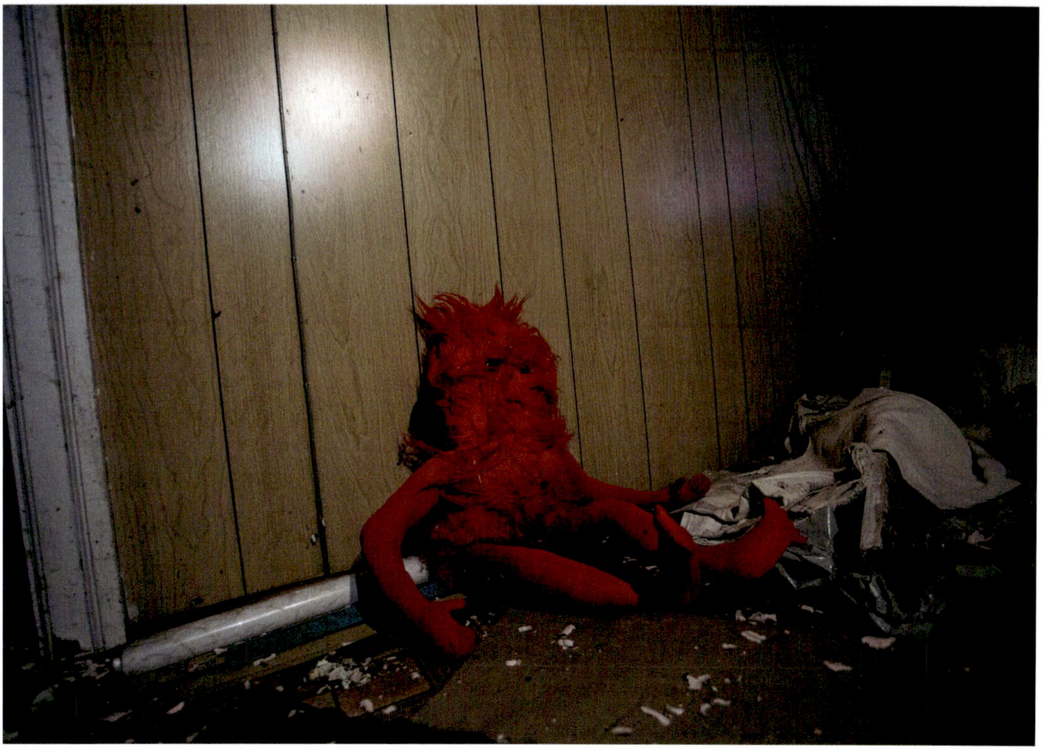

Stuffed animals and dolls from the past now seem like the things of nightmares.

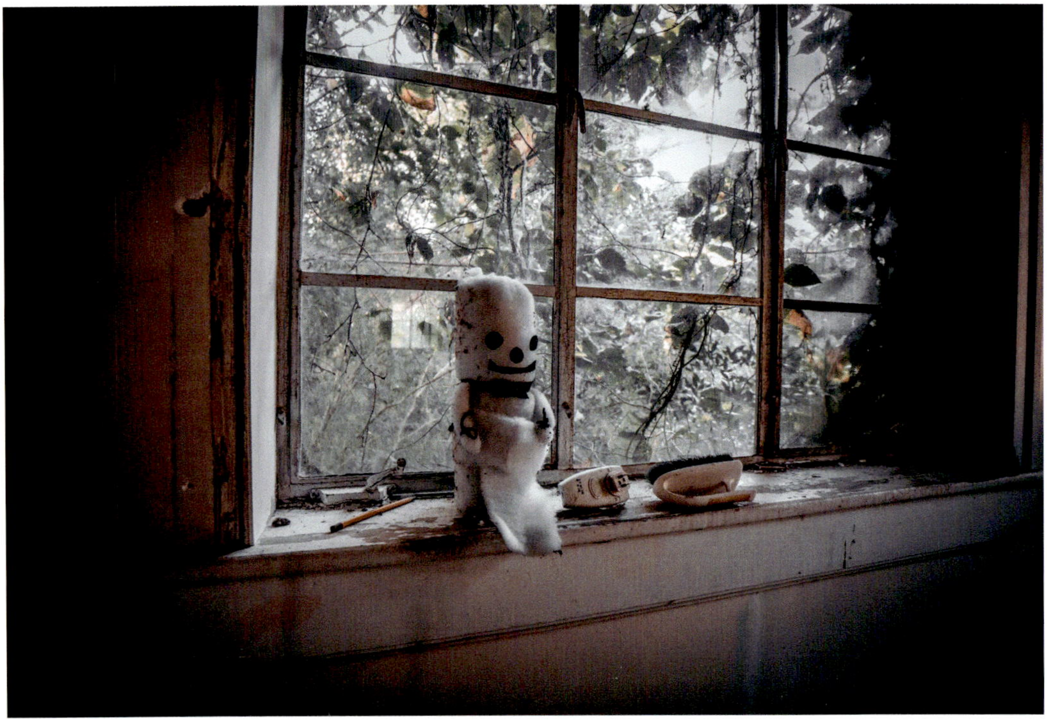

Small toys and stuffed animals in windows are another common sight in these abandoned homes.

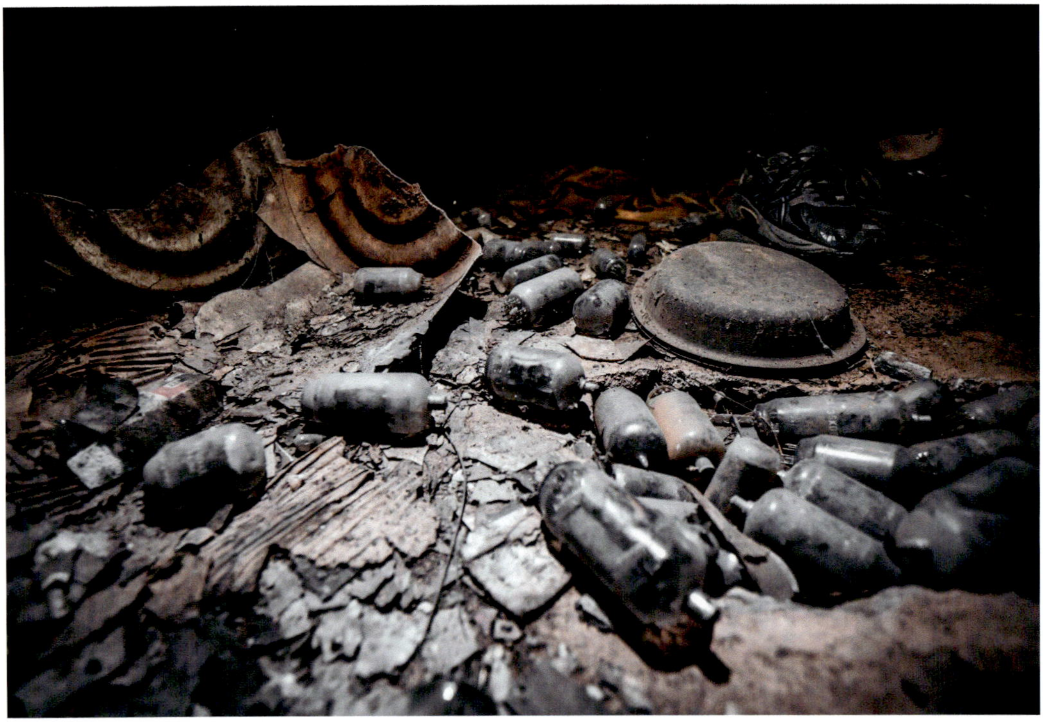

Electron tubes that were once utilized for old televisions, radios, and amplifiers are littered all over the floor of this old barn.

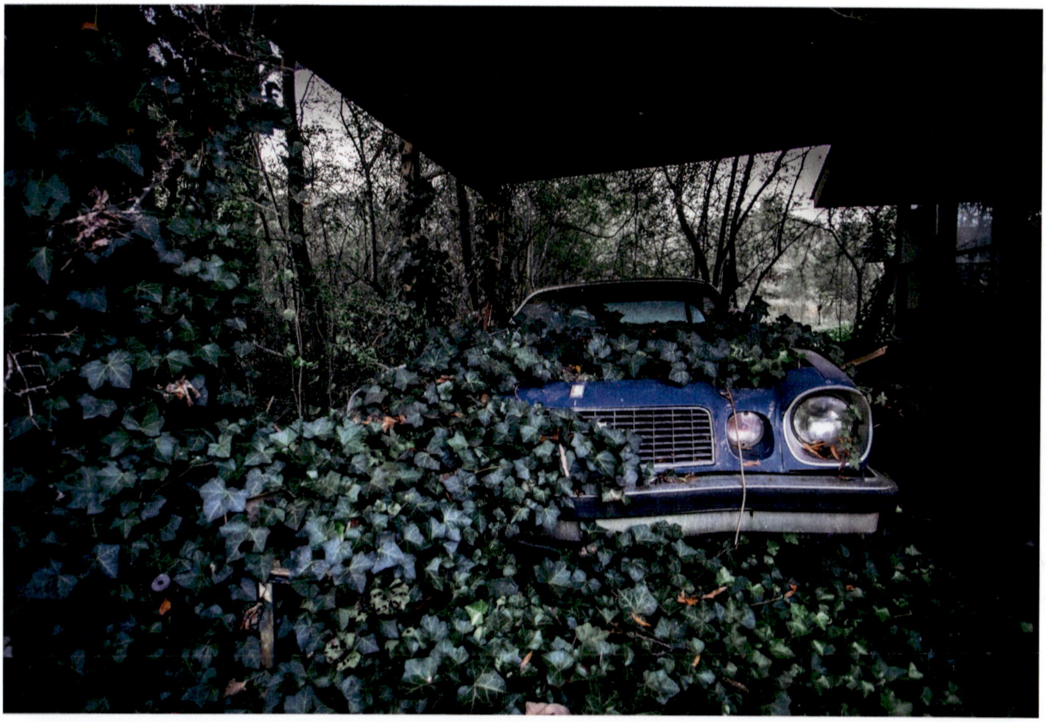

A vine-covered car left behind in a neighborhood with several abandoned homes.

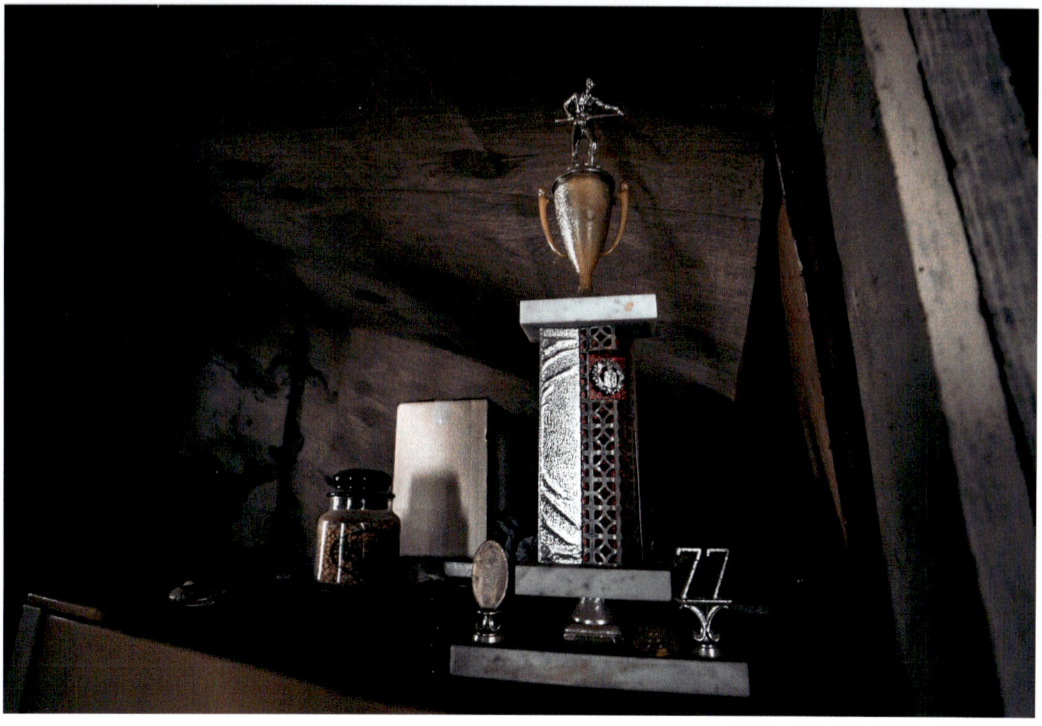

Trophies left behind are always sad to me. This one was still displayed on the refrigerator of a house abandoned in the 1980s.

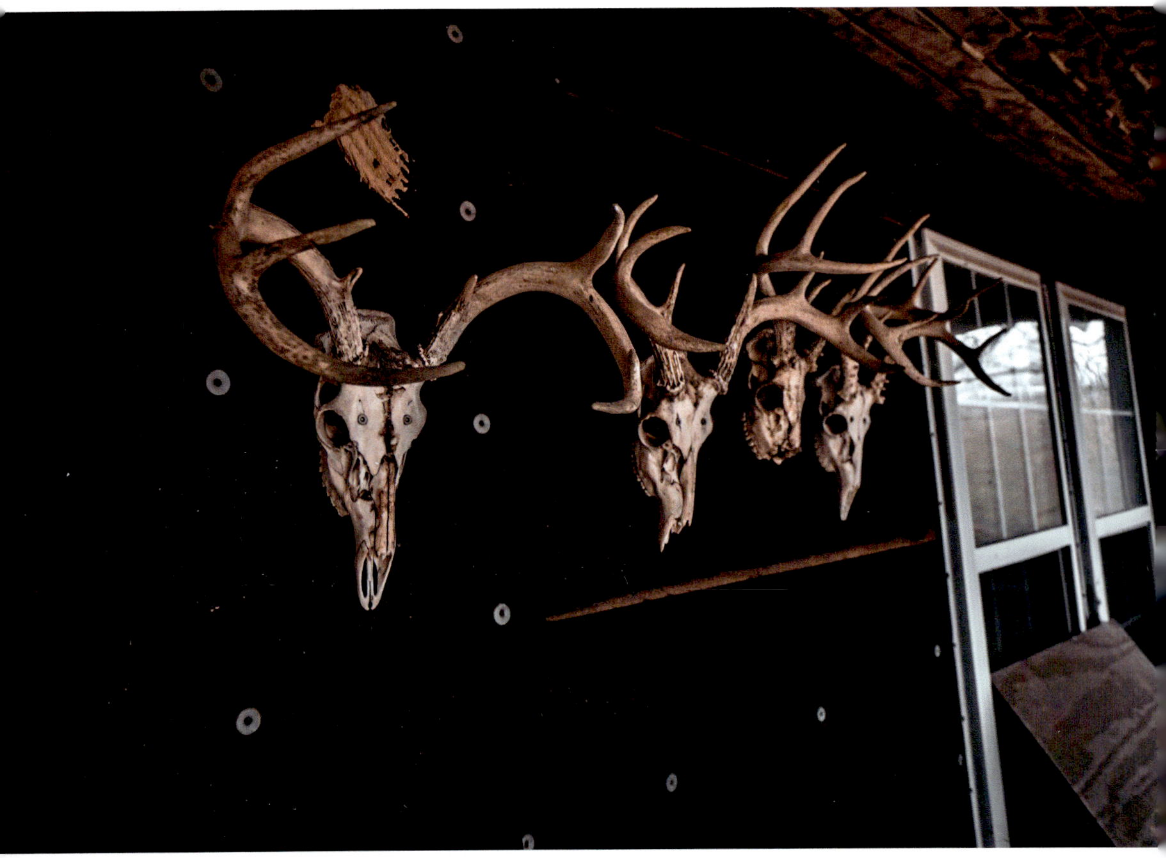

Proudly displayed deer skulls on an abandoned house.